SKILLS & VALUES:
CIVIL PROCEDURE

SKILLS & VALUES: CIVIL PROCEDURE

SECOND EDITION

Catherine Ross Dunham
Professor of Law
Elon University School of Law

Don C. Peters
University of Florida Levin College of Law
Former Director of Institute for Dispute Resolution; Trustee Research Fellow;
Professor Emeritus;
Former Associate Director, Center on Children and Families

 LexisNexis

ISBN: 978–0–7698–5496–0
eBook ISBN: 978–0–3271–8762–2

Library of Congress Cataloging-in-Publication Data

Dunham, Catherine Ross, author.
Skills & values. Civil procedure / Catherine Ross Dunham, Associate Dean of Academic Affairs, Professor of Law, Elon University School of Law; Don C. Peters, University of Florida Levin College of Law, Director of Institute for Dispute Resolution, Trustee Research Fellow, Professor; Associate Director, Center on Children and Families. -- Second edition.
pages cm. -- (Skills & values series)
No index.
ISBN 978-0-7698-5496-0
1. Civil procedure--United States--Problems, exercises, etc. I. Peters, Don C., 1944- author. II. Title. III. Title: Civil procedure. IV. Title: Skills and values.
KF8840.D86 2013
347.73'5--dc23
2013041110

NOTE TO USERS

To ensure that you are using the latest materials available in this area, please be sure to periodically check the LexisNexis Law School web site for downloadable updates and supplements at www.lexisnexis.com/lawschool.

Editorial Offices
121 Chanlon Rd., New Providence, NJ 07974 (908) 464-6800
201 Mission St., San Francisco, CA 94105-1831 (415) 908-3200
www.lexisnexis.com

MATTHEW◆BENDER

Introduction

The materials in this text were developed to assist students and instructors in incorporating legal skills and analytical skills into the substantive study of Civil Procedure. The materials are designed to allow students to apply the substantive material from class to practical problems and self-assess their own proficiency in understanding the topics while thinking analytically and practically about the law. Each chapter in this text addresses a fundamental topic area common to most first year Civil Procedure courses. The chapters include a short introduction of the topic area followed by a series of problems and exercises that address the analytical components of the topic. The goal of each topical chapter is not to reiterate the applicable rules of law as described in the course materials and by the professor. Rather, the focus of the materials is to provide students with opportunities to exercise analytical skills in the context of the relevant substantive law. Therefore, each chapter contains various exercises which seek to address key areas in each topic.

Many of the chapters in this text contain materials which can be accessed on the **LexisNexis Webcourse** that was created for this book. These materials may include client and witness instructions, additional factual summaries, analytical flow charts, podcasts, video materials, and links to other relevant materials. The text will prompt readers to access the online materials when the materials are relevant to the exercise.

The exercises are designed for student to perform a self-assessment, provided online, which provides detailed analysis of the exercises. These self-assessment materials are not *answers* to the exercises, they are offered as suggestions on how to analyze the fact situations in the exercises. Each student may reach a somewhat different conclusion on a given exercise, just as judges often reach different conclusions based on similar facts. The self-assessment materials are offered primarily as guides for students to develop and use analytical skills in the context of Civil Procedure.

Each chapter contains:

- An introduction that reviews the topic and introduces the exercise(s);
- One or more exercises on the topic;
- An estimated time for completing each exercise indicated by the icon below, each representing 15 minutes;

- An estimated degree of difficulty (difficult, moderate, easy) for each exercise represented by 1-5 black diamonds;

Dedication

Catherine would like to thank students and colleagues at the Elon University School of Law for their assistance in the preparation of this book. Also, Catherine humbly acknowledges the unending support of her family and dedicates this book to Jeff, Lucy and Davis.

Don dedicates this book to his wife, Martha M. Peters, and his sons, John D. Fitch, Michael L. Fitch, and Timothy D. Peters, with gratitude for the depth of appreciation of process, and the limits of attempts to regulate it, that loving them has given him.

Table of Contents

Table of Contents

Chapter 1

PERSONAL JURISDICTION: THE MINIMUM CONTACTS ANALYSIS

INTRODUCTION

Few things in the first semester of law school are as vexing as Civil Procedure, and, more specifically, the study of personal jurisdiction. Not only are you required to immerse yourself in a subject that celebrates a labyrinth of rules for civil litigation, but also you are expected to first learn the constitutional underpinnings of those rules. For this reason, the authors suggest you re-frame your understanding of how Civil Procedure is organized. First, understand that most Civil Procedure course designs include two courses, not one. The first course is a course in constitutional law, focusing primarily on Article III and the 14th Amendment to the Constitution. The second course is a course focused on a rule scheme, specifically the interrelated schematic of the Federal Rules of Civil Procedure. This distinction can help you work effectively, as law students need to read and work differently for a constitutional law course than they do for a statutory course. When you are studying personal jurisdiction, you are reading and working through your first constitutional law course.

The Constitutional Issue

Personal jurisdiction is a concept grounded in the procedural due process protections of the Constitution. In your Civil Procedure course, you most likely read the famous case, *Pennoyer v. Neff*,[1] which, in addition to its analysis of *in rem* and *in personam* jurisdiction, stands most importantly for the key constitutional principal in Civil Procedure: that personal jurisdiction is a protection given to defendants in civil litigation and guaranteed by the 5th and 14th Amendments of the Constitution. *Pennoyer*'s import flows from the Court's decision to place personal jurisdiction on the hard ground of the Constitution, thus allowing personal jurisdiction to stand side by side with the defendant's right to notice and an opportunity to be heard. After *Pennoyer*, a defendant in a civil suit could not be held to a judgment if she did not have notice of the suit or was not subject to the power of the court in the forum where the case was heard. If the court has no power over the defendant, any judgment against the defendant is not enforceable in the forum state or in other states under the Full Faith and Credit Clause.

The constitutional underpinning of personal jurisdiction explains why its study occupies so much of your class time and casebook. Making a mistake regarding the court's power over the defendant can nullify the entire action. Thus, understanding

---

[1] 95 U.S. 714 (1878).

personal jurisdiction is not just an academic undertaking but also an exercise in developing essential lawyering skills. The long line of cases that follow *Pennoyer* which work to define the parameters of the "minimum contacts test" create the framework for personal jurisdiction analysis.

Personal Jurisdiction Analysis: The Minimum Contacts Test

Understanding personal jurisdiction through case law can be tedious but the result is a working test for personal jurisdiction. Proper application of the test relies on your understanding of how and when it has been applied and when the test needs to be applied. You should always use your knowledge of the case law as a tool kit for analogic reasoning; comparing new facts to old cases. Also, you should develop your own framework for analyzing a personal jurisdiction problem. However, in any framework, the starting point should be analyzing the applicable long-arm statute.

To analyze whether the defendant is subject to personal jurisdiction, you first must determine if the defendant falls under the provisions of the applicable long-arm statute. For the most part, your study will focus on state long-arm statutes, although federal long-arm statutes do exist. Remember that in analyzing whether a defendant is subject to personal jurisdiction, the question asked is whether the defendant is subject to the power of the court in the forum. The term forum refers to the place where the case is brought. If the case is brought in New York state court, the forum is New York. If the case is brought in federal court in New York, the forum for purposes of analyzing personal jurisdiction is also New York. Thus, in both cases, the applicable question is whether the defendant falls within the New York long-arm statute.

Long-arm statutes generally follow one of two constructions: (1) statutes which allow personal jurisdiction over any defendant as long as consistent with the constitution and (2) statutes which identify specific situations which subject a defendant to personal jurisdiction in the forum. If the forum's long-arm statute refers to the constitutional rule, the statutory analysis merges with constitutional analysis, the "minimum contacts" analysis. If your case has a constitutionally based long-arm statute, analysis of the long-arm statute is not a separate test from the "minimum contacts" test. If the forum's long-arm statute addresses specific conduct which falls under the statute, such as entering into a contract with a resident of the forum, the defendant will either meet that conduct test or not. If the defendant did not engage in conduct included in the provisions of a specific act statute, the defendant will not be subject to personal jurisdiction in the forum. If the defendant did engage in conduct included in the provisions of the statute, the defendant will be subject to the personal jurisdiction of the forum, unless the statute itself legislates unconstitutionally.

After you have analyzed the role of the long-arm statute, the second step of the analysis is to identify the defendant's contacts with the forum. Contacts are factual happenings which demonstrate a connection with the forum. Contacts can be as extensive as owning a home or engaging in a business in the forum or as elusive as sending e-mail to a resident of the forum. The key is quality of contacts, not quantity of contacts. To analyze the contacts fully, you need to identify all the contacts and create a complete picture of the defendant's action in and with the forum.

The third analytical step is to analyze whether the defendant's contacts demonstrate purposeful availment. It is here that you are asking whether the defendant's contacts with the forum subject him to the power of the forum. Under the heading of purposeful availment, you will employ different approaches depending on the facts of the defendant's contacts. Some appropriate questions in this part of the analysis include:

- Are the defendant's contacts purposeful? In other words, do the contacts demonstrate the defendant's intent to take advantage of the benefits and protections of the forum state?

- Does the defendant manufacture a product which traveled into the forum state? Does the defendant manufacture a component part of another product which traveled into the forum state?

- Do the defendant's actions constitute an intentional tort having an effect within the forum state?

In considering purposeful availment, you must also analyze whether the defendant's contacts in the forum state are related to the lawsuit? In some cases, the defendant's contacts in the forum are so pervasive, any lawsuit against the defendant in the forum passes the relatedness test. These situations are somewhat rare, but you may have studied cases such as *Perkins v. Benguet Consol. Mining Co.*[2] or *Helicopteros Nacionales de Columbia, S.A. v. Hall*[3] which address the concept of general jurisdiction. In cases where general jurisdiction is not at issue, the defendant may have narrow contacts with the forum. In those cases, cases of specific jurisdiction, the lawsuit must relate to the defendant's contacts in the forum in order for the defendant to be subjected to personal jurisdiction in the forum.

After considering the long-arm statute, the defendant's contacts in the forum, and the purposeful availment questions, the personal jurisdiction analysis shifts. The final question in the analysis is whether taking personal jurisdiction over the defendant is fair and reasonable. Since the concept of personal jurisdiction is rooted in the 14th Amendment, the court must assess whether it is fair to hail the defendant into a foreign court. If the court determines the exercise of personal jurisdiction is unfair to the defendant, the defendant will not be required to answer the lawsuit in that forum. In assessing fairness, the court analyzes fairness factors, also known as the Gestalt factors, which include:

- the fairness to the defendant;

- the fairness to the plaintiff;

- the interest of the forum state; and

- the interest of other states.

Some courts also consider the effect of a particular court's actions on interstate justice as part of the fairness analysis. Courts may also consider the fairness factors in various orders and balance the factors differently, depending on the facts of the case.

---

[2] 342 U.S. 437 (1952).

[3] 466 U.S. 408 (1984).

Once you have walked through the requisite steps of the personal jurisdiction analysis, you are ready to advise on whether the defendant is subject to the power of the court in the forum state. Remember that this question is fundamental to effective civil litigation and must be analyzed not only defensively, but also by the plaintiff before a forum is chosen and suit is filed. Failure to properly assess whether the court has personal jurisdiction over the defendant can lead a plaintiff to incur costs and devote time to a lawsuit wherein even a victory could lead to an unenforceable judgment.

EXERCISE 1: THE BOSWELL SCHOOL

FOCUS OF THIS EXERCISE: The Minimum Contacts Analysis.

SKILLS INVOLVED: Developing and evaluating the arguments of both sides; using an analytical framework to review the relevant facts of the problem in the context of the procedural question; weighing the arguments from the trial court's point of view.

ESTIMATED TIME FOR COMPLETING THE EXERCISE: One to two hours

LEVEL OF DIFFICULTY: Moderate

YOUR ROLE IN THIS EXERCISE: You are playing the role of the Judge in this exercise. The defendant has asked the trial court to dismiss the case on grounds that the Texas trial court does not have personal jurisdiction over the defendant. You must consider each side's argument on issues of minimum contacts and purposeful availment then make a ruling. You should read the fact summary then (1) create an outline of the relevant analysis; (2) map out the arguments for both sides; and, (3) write out a short Order stating the decision of the trial court and the grounds for the decision.

The Boswell School, a private boarding school for boys located in the Blue Ridge Mountains of central Virginia, specializes in educating and treating teenagers with emotional and psychological problems. Many of the students have been kicked out of other schools. The school is incorporated in Virginia, where it has a principal place of business. The cost for an academic year at the school is $50,000. There are a total of 100 students in the school which covers grades 9 through 12. The majority of the students come from the Virginia, Maryland, and the Washington D.C. areas, with some from various other states. Four Texas students have attended Boswell over the last decade (prior to Peter Smith's attending, as described below). The school staff includes psychologists, as well as a psychiatrist who is a medical doctor and can prescribe medication to students. The Smiths, who live in Houston, Texas, sent their teenage son Peter to the Boswell School after he was kicked out of a private school in Houston for drug possession and threatening a teacher with a gun. The Smiths found out about Boswell from an advertisement in the New York Times Magazine, which is distributed nationally with the Sunday New York Times. The Smiths contacted the school, which sent them a DVD about Boswell. The Smiths later visited the school, and then made arrangements by mail for Peter to attend.

After Peter had attended Boswell for a semester and shortly before Peter left to go home for Christmas break, the school psychiatrist prescribed a new anti-depressant, Elixir, for Peter. While Peter was home for the holidays, he snorted some cocaine. Perhaps due to the interaction of Elixir and cocaine, Peter suffered a psychotic episode during which he jumped from a second story window of his parents' Houston home. Peter's jump resulted in serious fractures to both of his legs, which will incapacitate him for six months and possibly affect him for life.

Peter (through his parents) sues the Boswell School in the federal court for the Southern District of Texas, claiming that his personal injuries were caused by the malpractice of the school's psychiatrist in giving him a new medication without monitoring its effects. The Boswell School has filed a timely motion under Rule 12(b)(2) arguing that there is no personal jurisdiction.

The state long arm statute provides, in relevant part, for jurisdiction "a court of this state may exercise jurisdiction on any basis not inconsistent with the Constitution of this state or of the United States."

LexisNexis Webcourse for Exercise 1:

Access the Minimum Contacts Flow Chart on the **LexisNexis Webcourse** that was created for this book and use it to organize your analysis of the Boswell exercise. You may also want to access the Review Podcast on Minimum Contacts which is also available on the **LexisNexis Webcourse** that was created for this book.

Chapter 2

SUBJECT MATTER JURISDICTION

INTRODUCTION

As we noted in the Introduction to Chapter 1, a Civil Procedure course is really two courses in one; a course in constitutional law and a course in statutory law. The jurisdictional topics are key components of the constitutional law portion of your Civil Procedure course. Both jurisdictional topics examine the power of the court to render an enforceable judgment. Personal jurisdiction examines the court's power over the person and subject matter jurisdiction examines the court's power over the case. This chapter addresses the law and analysis for subject matter jurisdiction.

The term subject matter jurisdiction refers to the court's constitutional power to hear a particular case. If the court lacks subject matter jurisdiction over the case, the court has no power over the case and cannot issue rulings enforceable against the parties. Federal court subject matter jurisdiction arises from Article III, Section 2 of the Constitution which outlines the type of cases a federal court has the power to hear. The two Article III, Section 2 sub-sections relevant to the materials in this Chapter are: (1) ". . . all cases, in law and equity, arising under this Constitution, the laws of the United States . . .", and (2) ". . . controversies between two or more states; — between a state and citizens of another state; — between citizens of different states . . . ." These constitutional provisions were codified into Chapter 28 of the United States Code. The federal statute which authorizes federal courts to hear cases involving disputes arising under the laws of the United States is 28 U.S.C. § 1331. The federal statute which authorizes federal courts to hear cases involving disputes between citizens of different states is 28 U.S.C. § 1332.

Subject Matter Jurisdiction based on a Federal Question

Federal question subject matter jurisdiction, which was codified in 28 U.S.C. § 1331, allows federal courts to hear cases when federal law governs the dispute. In many cases, it is not difficult to determine that a federal court has subject matter jurisdiction based on a federal question, such as in a civil rights action brought under 42 U.S.C. § 1983. In this type of case, the statute that gives rise to the plaintiff's claim is a federal statute. Thus, the claim is said to be "created" by federal law. In other cases, the plaintiff's claim involves both federal and state law, such as when a trucking company violates federal safety laws which leads to an accident and a negligence claim by an injured plaintiff. In that type of case, the court must determine whether the federal safety law is an "essential federal ingredient" of the plaintiff's negligence claim. If the court determines that the federal law is an essential ingredient of the state law claim, the federal court will have subject matter jurisdiction over the case and the case can be heard in federal court.

The federal question analysis can be quite complicated, especially if an essential federal ingredient question is raised. The rules are stated succinctly here, as this text assumes you have covered this material in your Civil Procedure course.

Subject Matter Jurisdiction based on Diversity of Citizenship

Diversity-based subject matter jurisdiction, which was codified in 28 U.S.C. § 1332, applies when the dispute arises under state law and involves a controversy between citizens from different states.[1] Determining whether the court has subject matter jurisdiction over a case based on diversity of citizenship involves two main inquiries. First, the court must determine whether the claims asserted by the plaintiff meet the amount in controversy requirement of 28 U.S.C. § 1332. Under the current statute, the plaintiff's claim must constitute a good faith allegation that the claim asserted is worth more than $75,000, exclusive of fees and costs. If the plaintiff's claim does not meet this amount, the federal court does not have the power to hear the case. Second, the federal courts have the power to hear a case (which meets the amount in controversy) if the case involves a dispute between parties who are citizens of different states. For example, if a plaintiff from Nebraska brings suit against a defendant from Idaho, the parties are considered diverse and the federal court will have subject matter jurisdiction over the case as long as the amount in controversy is met. The courts have interpreted the diversity requirement to be limited to cases with complete diversity, wherein every plaintiff is diverse from every defendant. Under this interpretation, the federal court will not be able to hear the case if any parties on opposite sides of the "v" are from the same state. Always remember that for a federal court to have subject matter jurisdiction over a case based on diversity of citizenship, both the amount in controversy and complete diversity requirements must be met.

Analyzing Subject Matter Jurisdiction

When analyzing whether the court has subject matter jurisdiction over a case based on either federal question or diversity of citizenship, focus on these important points. First, remember that any person, including the court, can raise challenges to subject matter jurisdiction at any time. The fact that a federal court makes a mistaken judgment on its subject matter jurisdiction or a party fails to challenge subject matter jurisdiction does not waive the inquiry. If the case is improperly before the court, the court lacks the power to hear the case thus the case can be dismissed at any time, even on appeal. An analysis which concludes that a party has waived her challenge to subject matter jurisdiction is never correct or complete.

The subject matter jurisdiction inquiry examines whether the case can be heard in federal court, not whether the case can be heard in another court. The fact that a federal court cannot hear the case does not mean the case cannot be heard in an appropriate state court. If a plaintiff files her case in federal court based on diversity

---

[1] Note that the actual text of Article III, Section 2 and 28 U.S.C. § 1332 applies to more types of controversies than only those between citizens of different states. The intro text here focuses on only one type of diversity controversy.

of citizenship but fails to meet the amount in controversy requirement, the case will be dismissed from federal court only. The plaintiff may still be able to bring the case in an appropriate state court.

Diagrams are very helpful when analyzing subject matter jurisdiction. When reading a set of facts about a civil case, it is worth your time to create a diagram noting the names and positions of the parties, the citizenship of the parties, the nature of the claims involved, and the amount in controversy. In a case where Mr. and Mrs. Jones from Nebraska sue Star Trucking, Inc., John Smith (the truck driver), and AAA Maintenance (the company servicing the truck), all from Idaho, seeking $250,000 in damages for negligence related to an accident in Nebraska, the diagram might be as follows:

Negligence; $250,000

Mrs. Jones (Neb.)   Star Trucking, Inc. (Idaho)
Mr. Jones (Neb.)   v.   John Smith (Idaho)
                                     AAA Maintenance (Idaho)

Subject matter jurisdiction, like personal jurisdiction, relies on constitutional principles, thus the analysis requires a subtle hand and an ability to parse out the relevant facts. When considering subject matter jurisdiction, start by examining the legal basis of the claim; state law, federal law or some combination. Also, in federal question cases, consider the legal claims as noted in the plaintiff's complaint. For the claim to arise under federal law, the federal claim must be included in the plaintiff's complaint, not in the defendant's answer or another responsive pleading.[2]

The following exercise is designed to help you evaluate your understanding of the analysis for subject matter jurisdiction, focusing more specifically on subject matter jurisdiction based on diversity of citizenship. In this exercise you are asked to create an office memorandum for the supervising partner analyzing the subject matter jurisdiction issue. Before beginning your analysis, consider first making a diagram of the case like the example above.

---

[2] *See Louisville & Nashville Railway Co. v. Mottley*, 211 U.S. 149 (1908).

EXERCISE 1: DR. VAGO'S INVESTMENT

FOCUS OF THIS EXERCISE: This exercise is designed to test your knowledge of subject matter jurisdiction and your ability to analyze a fact situation involving the applicable rules of law. In completing this exercise, you should focus on marshaling the facts, as related by the client, into a set of facts you can analyze.

SKILLS INVOLVED: Understanding the relevant facts as related by the client; using an analytical framework to review the relevant facts in the context of the procedural question; developing an argument framework for your client based on the relevant law.

ESTIMATED TIME FOR COMPLETING THIS EXERCISE: One to two hours

ESTIMATED LEVEL OF DIFFICULTY: Moderate

YOUR ROLE IN THIS EXERCISE: In this exercise, you represent Dr. Vago. He has come to your supervising attorney for advice on pursuing an action against Martin and Speak Easy. You have been asked to consider whether Dr. Vago can bring his suit against Martin and Speak Easy in federal district court. Assume your supervising attorney has met with Dr. Vago and created the following memo which relates the facts about Vago's involvement with Martin and Speak Easy. To enable you to focus here on subject matter jurisdiction only, assume issues of personal jurisdiction have been resolved and other associates also working on the case will handle other matters. Please visit the **LexisNexis Webcourse** to see the text of the relevant statute and to view a video interview for this exercise.

NOTE TO READERS: The Dr. Vago's Investment exercise can also be used to analyze personal jurisdiction. If using this exercise for personal jurisdiction, ask whether Dr. Vago can sue Martin and Speak Easy in federal court in Alabama.

EXERCISE 1:   DR. VAGO'S INVESTMENT

Memorandum
To: Associate
From: Supervising Attorney
Re: *Vago v. Martin and Speak Easy*; File No. 1234-0009

Dr. G. Vago, a client of the firm, believes he was defrauded on a real estate investment agreement he made two years ago. This agreement concerned a development in Cook County, Illinois, called Capstone Estates. Capstone Estates is a real estate development undertaken by the Speak Easy Development Corporation, an entity incorporated in Delaware with its principal place of business in Chicago, Illinois. The President, Chief Executive Officer, and sole shareholder of Speak Easy Development Corp. is Rick Martin.

Dr. Vago met Martin at a professional meeting for cardiac physicians in the Southeastern United States held at Sea Island, Georgia, in September yr-3.[3] Vago was one of six Alabama physicians attending the meeting. During the three-day meeting, Martin was a panelist at a session regarding investment strategies. Martin pitched real estate opportunities as great investments for doctors with cash on hand. Vago attended Martin's open session on real estate investing. After the session, Vago approached Martin and talked with Martin about Capstone Estates and other real estate investment ideas. The two men talked for about thirty minutes and Vago took materials on Capstone Estates, which Martin made available to all the meeting participants who approached his display on Capstone Estates. Dr. Vago did not make any commitment to Martin or Capstone Estates at the Sea Island meeting. The two men did, however, exchange business cards.

When Dr. Vago returned to Birmingham, he reviewed some of the information on Capstone Estates and decided to contact Martin about investing. Dr. Vago called Martin and asked for information. Martin responded by mailing a brochure and prospectus describing the financial benefits of an investment in Capstone Estates. Dr. Vago then placed a call to Martin to ask questions about the materials on Capstone Estates. Martin, at Dr. Vago's request, faxed a contract to Vago in Alabama for investing in Capstone Estates.

Two days after receiving the faxed contract, Dr. Vago called Martin and orally agreed to buy into Capstone Estates. The terms in this faxed contract provided an entry price of $500,000. This investment amount entitled Dr. Vago to receive 7% of all net profits earned from the development and sale of town homes on Capstone Estates. The contract also provided that "this agreement shall be governed in accordance with the laws of the State of Illinois."

Dr. Vago signed the contract on October 6, yr-3 and sent it to Martin, along with a

---

[3] yr-3 indicates that the year dated is three years ago from the current date. For example if you are working on this exercise in 2014, Dr. Vago went to Sea Island in March 2011.

$500,000 personal check drawn on Dr. Vago's Alabama bank. Banking records show that five days later, on October 11, yr-3, Martin cashed Dr. Vago's check.

After one year, Dr. Vago had not received any profits from his $500,000 investment into Capstone Estates. In October yr-2, Dr. Vago began to write Martin at the Speak Easy office address in Chicago and demand information on his investment. He wrote three letters to Martin demanding information, each letter sent by certified mail. An unidentified person in Speak Easy's office signed for each letter but no one responded to Dr. Vago's letters. Dr. Vago also called Martin ten times between October yr-2 and January yr-1, requesting information on Capstone Estates. In these ten calls, Dr. Vago spoke with Martin only once, all other times leaving messages with Martin's assistant. In February yr-1, Dr. Vago finally contacted the Chicago Area Development Commission to get information on Capstone Estates. Through several phone calls, Dr. Vago learned that Capstone Estates was delayed indefinitely due to problems with permitting. Dr. Vago also learned that Martin and Speak Easy had been sued for fraud in six other states for matters related to Capstone Estates.

Dr. Vago believes he was defrauded by Martin and Speak Easy and wants to do whatever it takes to get his money back. He has asked us to represent him in a lawsuit against Martin and Speak Easy. **Please analyze whether Vago can bring his case in federal district court in either Alabama or Illinois.**

Put your analysis into the form of an office memorandum using the following heading

Memorandum

To: Supervising Attorney
From: Associate

Re: *Vago v. Martin and Speak Easy*; File No. 1234-0009

Web Course for Exercise 1:   Dr. Vago's Investment

Access the **LexisNexis Webcourse** to review the client interview video for this problem. You may also want to review the Subject Matter Jurisdiction Flow Chart and listen to the Subject Matter Jurisdiction Review Podcast before creating your memorandum to the supervising attorney.

Chapter 3

THE NOTICE REQUIREMENT

INTRODUCTION

The topic of notice is the third topic in the constitutional portion of your Civil Procedure course. Notice refers principally to the process of letting the defendant know that a civil lawsuit is pending against her. If the defendant does not have notice of the lawsuit, she is not able to appear in court and defend her position. Therefore, proper notice is an essential ingredient in an enforceable judgment. If a court hears a case when notice to the defendant has been inadequate or defective, any ruling in the case is subject to challenge on constitutional grounds.

The notice requirement is often discussed in the context of the rule-based requirement for service of process. Service of legal process is the mechanism for accomplishing notice and requires the lawsuit be served on the defendant through a process specified under the applicable rules. Rule 4 of the Federal Rules of Civil Procedure is the statutory section which specifies how the plaintiff should deliver notice to the defendant in cases pending in federal district court. For the notice requirement to be met, the plaintiff must comply with the technical specifications of Rule 4 in delivering notice to the defendant. If the notice fails technically, it fails overall. Also, actual knowledge is not a substitute for proper notice. If a plaintiff makes a technical error in serving notice on the defendant, for example by leaving the notice at the defendant's home with a child, not a person over 18 years of age, the fact that the defendant received and read the notice does not cure the technical defect. The notice must be properly served under the applicable rule regardless of the defendant's actual knowledge of the lawsuit.

Not only does the plaintiff have to comply with the technical specifics of the applicable rule, the rule itself must conform to the constitutional requirements for adequate notice. The Constitution requires that notice, and the statutory parameters for providing notice, must be reasonably calculated to inform the interested parties of the pending action.[1] To be constitutional, the form of notice must meet this standard. For example, if the plaintiff knows the current address of the defendant, he cannot provide her notice through newspaper publication instead of providing notice by in-person service or mail. Since service by newspaper publication may not reach the defendant it is not reasonably calculated to inform the defendant of the pending action when other better means are available. In this example, a statute may allow for notice through newspaper publication but that fact alone does not ensure the notice, as executed, is constitutionally proper. The notice can be challenged on constitutional

---

[1] *See Mullane v. Central Hanover Bank & Trust Co.*, 399 U.S. 306 (1950).

grounds even in cases where the plaintiff followed the statutory requirements if the statutory requirements are constitutionally inadequate.

Notice issues arise when service is either technically inept or the notice does meet the "reasonably calculated" standard. The examples which follow are intended to help you understand the notice requirement more completely. When reviewing the materials, try to first determine whether the issue relates to technical compliance or problems with the statutory scheme for notice. Also, remember that actual knowledge is never a substitute for proper notice.

EXERCISE 1: THE MORENO FAMILY

FOCUS OF THIS EXERCISE: Understanding the *Mullane* standard for notice reasonably calculated to apprise the defendant of the pending action.

SKILLS INVOLVED: Developing and evaluating the arguments of both sides; utilizing precedent and a legal standard in a factual analysis; evaluating policy arguments.

ESTIMATED TIME FOR COMPLETING THE EXERCISE: One hour

ESTIMATED LEVEL OF DIFFICULTY: Moderate to easy

YOUR ROLE IN THIS EXERCISE: You are serving in the role of the reviewing court in this exercise. The administrative agency has issued an order in favor of the City and the City has evicted the Moreno family. The Moreno family argues the eviction is not enforceable because the notice of the eviction action was inadequate. The City argues the notice was reasonably calculated to apprise the Morenos of the pending eviction action. You must consider each side's argument on issues then make a determination on the notice issue in the form of a court Order with findings of fact and conclusions of law. In completing this assignment, you should (1) review the problem and the relevant precedent; (2) outline the arguments for the Morenos and the City; (3) make a determination of the issue based on the law and the facts; and (4) create an Order stating your findings and conclusions.

Note that the relevant precedent is accessible through the **LexisNexis Webcourse** that was created for this book. Also note that a template for the Order is on the **LexisNexis Webcourse** that was created for this book. You should use the electronic template to craft your Order.

EXERCISE 1: THE MORENO FAMILY

Isidro Moreno and his family legally immigrated to the United States from Mexico five years ago. As part of a New York City housing program, Isidro and his family qualified for a rent-controlled apartment in a City housing project designed to meet the needs of Latino immigrants. The apartment complex contains 60 units, all housing immigrant families who speak Spanish as their primary language. Many of the families do not include an English-speaking member of the family. Thus, the signs posted in the complex are all in Spanish, the City officials assigned to manage the project are all fluent in Spanish, and the complex is located in a predominantly Latino neighborhood served by a Spanish immersion public school.

Several years after moving into the City complex, Isidro lost his job and became unemployed. To earn money for his family, he accepted a number of odd jobs while he looked for permanent work. During this down time, Isidro fell behind on his rent and the City initiated an eviction action against him in accordance with the statutory provisions regarding the public housing complex. In accordance with the statute, the City mailed notice to Isidro using certified mail and served him personally at his home in the complex. The eviction action was handled by the City's legal office, not the Latino complex managers. The notice was in English and the process server did not speak Spanish. Isidro called the Latino complex managers but was told they did not manage eviction actions and could not help him. They directed him to the City's legal department. When Isidro contacted the City's legal department, he was unable to get information about the papers he received because no one at the legal department spoke Spanish.

Several weeks later, the New York Public Housing Agency issued an Order of Eviction against Isidro and the City evicted his family from their apartment.

Isidro and his family have appealed the Agency Eviction Order to the reviewing court arguing the notice was inadequate under the standards for adequate notice set forth in *Mullane v. Central Hanover Bank & Trust Co.* and *Mennonite Board of Missions v. Adams.*

Webcourse for Exercise 1:

Access the Order Template on the **LexisNexis Webcourse** that was created for this book and use it to organize your analysis of the Moreno problem.

The authority for this exercise is *Mullane v. Central Hanover Bank & Trust Co.* and *Mennonite Board of Missions v. Adams*. Please use the links on the LexisNexis web course that was created for this book to access these cases.

CASE BRIEF:
MULLANE v. CENTRAL HANOVER BANK & TRUST CO.,
339 U.S. 306 (1950).

In 1946, Central Hanover Bank & Trust Co. established a common trust fund for investors, a precursor to the modern day mutual fund. Under New York law, the trustees were required to file periodic accountings reporting the management of the trust income and assets to the beneficiaries. If the beneficiaries failed to contest the accounting within a specific time, the beneficiaries forfeited their legal right to bring claims regarding the management of the trust fund. When the Bank filed an accounting in New York Surrogate's Court in 1947, the only notice given to the beneficiaries of the trust fund's proposed accounting was through publication in a local newspaper, which ran once each week for four consecutive weeks. This notice by local publication was the notice required under New York law.

When the trust beneficiaries failed to receive notice of the accounting proceeding in time to contest the trust's management, they filed suit arguing notice by publication was improper. The case came to the Supreme Court on review of the constitutionality of the New York statute allowing notice by publication. The facts showed that the Bank had the names and addresses of all the beneficiaries on hand but did not mail notice, relying instead only on publication notice. The Court held that publication notice was not inadequate notice in situations where the identity or the location of the person being sought was unknown; however, held whether notice was proper depended on the surrounding circumstances. In *Mullane*, the identities of all the beneficiaries were known to the Bank, and the beneficiaries could have easily been informed of the accounting proceeding by mail. Moreover, the Bank had routinely communicated with the trust beneficiaries through mail, thus the beneficiaries were accustomed to receiving information from the Bank by mail.

The Court ruled in favor of the trust beneficiaries, holding that when a pending action will affect an interest in life, liberty or property protected by the 14th Amendment to the Constitution, a State must provide "notice reasonably calculated, under all the circumstances, to apprise interested parties of the pendency of the action and afford them an opportunity to present their objections." In the *Mullane* case, the New York statute failed to meet this constitutional test, thus the notice given by the Bank to the beneficiaries per the statute was inadequate.

CASE BRIEF:
MENNONITE BOARD OF MISSIONS v. ADAMS,
462 U.S. 791 (1983).

In 1973, Ms. Alfred Jean Moore took out a mortgage secured by her real property. The Mennonite Board of Missions (MBM) held the $14,000 mortgage with a secured interest in Ms. Moore's real property. Under the terms of the loan, Ms. Moore was obligated to pay the taxes on the real estate. When she failed to do so, Elkhart County, Indiana instituted proceedings to sell Ms. Moore's property for payment of the taxes. The County followed the statutory guidelines for notice by posting notice of the tax sale in the County courthouse and mailing notice to Ms. Moore. The County did not give notice to MBM despite the fact that the mortgage naming MBM as the lender was on file in the County public records. The property was sold to Adams for the amount of taxes owed and MBM was uninformed and unaware of the sale. Ms. Moore continued to pay her mortgage to MBM for two years after the tax sale so MBM was not aware of the transfer of the property until 1979 when the buyer, Adams, filed suit to quiet title to the real estate. MBM argued that because they did not receive proper notice of the tax sale, they had not waived their interest in the property. The case went to the United States Supreme Court on the constitutional challenge to the Indiana state statute on notice.

In reviewing the Indiana statute, the Court relied on its decision in *Mullane v. Central Hanover Bank & Trust Co.*, 339 U.S. 306 (1950), which held that notice must be reasonably calculated to apprise interested parties of the pendency of the action and afford them an opportunity to present objections. The Court held that when the mortgage lender was identifiable through the County records, notice by publication was not reasonable. The Court ruled the Indiana notice statute unconstitutional, finding that the County's use of a less reliable form of notice, such as publication, was not reasonable when an "inexpensive and efficient mechanism such as mail service is available."

Sample Order for The Moreno Problem

IN THE GENERAL COURT OF JUSTICE
SUPREME COURT DIVISION; PART V

NEW YORK COUNTY   09 CVD 12548

NEW YORK COUNTY
CITY OF NEW YORK PUBLIC
HOUSING AGENCY,
                     PLAINTIFF,   ORDER OF EVICTION
          vs.
ISIDRO MORENO,
                     DEFENDANT.

THIS MATTER was heard by the Undersigned Judge Presiding over the 20_____ Civil Session of the Supreme Court Division, Part V, upon complaint of Plaintiff for eviction.

BASED upon matters of record, the Court makes the following:

FINDINGS OF FACT

1. Plaintiff is the City of New York Public Housing Agency and is located in New York County, New York.

2. Defendant Isidro Moreno, is a citizen and resident of New York County, New York, and has been a resident of the State of New York for at least six months preceding the institution of this action.

3. Defendant resides with his family in a rent-controlled apartment which is part of a City housing project designed to meet the needs of Latino immigrants.

4. The apartment complex contains 60 units. All residents speak Spanish as their primary language.

5. All signs posted within the complex are in Spanish. The complex is located in a Latino neighborhood served by a Spanish immersion school.

6. Defendant lost his job after several years of employment and was unable to continue paying rent, at which point Plaintiff initiated an eviction proceeding against him.

7. Defendant was served personally with notice of eviction for non-payment of rent. The notice was in English and the process server did not speak Spanish.

8. Defendant attempted to work with the Spanish speaking complex managers, but was told they did not handle eviction matters. Defendant subsequently called the City's legal department, but was unable to speak with anyone who

spoke Spanish.

9. In accordance with the New York City ordinance number 789-18564, the Plaintiff Agency evicted Defendant and his family from their apartment for non-payment of rent.

Based upon the foregoing Findings of Fact, the Court CONCLUDES AS A MATTER OF LAW: (To complete the exercise, fill in this section with numbered conclusions of law based on the applicable law.)

IT IS, THEREFORE, ORDERED, ADJUDGED AND DECREED: (To complete this exercise, fill in this section with the appropriate decision based on your analysis.)

More Exercises on the Notice Requirement

What follows are two additional short exercises on the topic of service of process incorporating the *Mullane* standard and Federal Rule 4. Before attempting these exercises, review *Mullane* and Rule 4. Next, read the exercise and write out your analysis, using either an outline or a narrative form, before reviewing the analysis included on the **LexisNexis Webcourse**. Consider using the information in the analysis created for Exercise 2 to revise your written work before moving on to Exercise 3 of this Chapter.

EXERCISE 2: THE MISSING DEFENDANT

Problem: What should the party do when service by mail does not work? Assume you send notice by certified or registered mail to several addresses found through investigation and receive no signed responses. What should the lawyer do in a case where the defendant's whereabouts are completely unknown even after investigation? For this exercise, assume the case is filed in Federal District Court and the Federal Rules of Civil Procedure apply.

EXERCISE 3: SERVICE BY PUBLICATION

Problem: You live in New York City and are suing someone for breach of contract. You have tried diligently to locate this person and have tried and failed at personal and mail service. Under the rules, you can still give proper notice by publishing the action in a newspaper of general circulation in the area where the lawsuit is filed. The New York Times charges $1,000.00 for each run of a legal advertisement and you must run the ad four consecutive times. However, the Brooklyn Advocate, a small paper targeted at people of a certain political persuasion living in Brooklyn, will run the ad four times for $100. Does it matter in which paper you run the ad if both are accessible in the federal district where the lawsuit is filed?

More Practice on Service of Process

Many professors use multiple-choice questions to test certain topics covered within the first year Civil Procedure course. Although essay questions allow students time and space to fully develop analysis, multiple-choice questions provide a very strong method of assessing the student's understanding of the core material and the student's ability to analyze the question. Also, because the Multi-State Bar Examination consists entirely of multiple-choice questions, it is wise for students to begin practicing their skill at analysis through a multiple-choice question in the first year of law school.

The following questions are designed to test a student's understanding of the rules from *Mullane* and *Mennonite Board of Missions*. The questions are in multiple-choice format and the student is instructed to select the **best** answer from the choices given. In this type of multiple-choice question, there may be more than one correct answer to the question. The student's task is to analyze the fact pattern in the question and select the **best** answer.

Consider using this exercise to practice for examinations by simulating an exam experience and limiting your time to 15 minutes, 5 minutes per question. The best answer to the question and an evaluation of each question can be found on the **LexisNexis Webcourse**.

EXERCISE 4: MOCK EXAM ON SERVICE OF PROCESS

Freddie Locke failed to pay the City of Monroesville property taxes on the house in which he was living. The City sued in state court to foreclose on the house in payment of the overdue City taxes. In accordance with the state statute specifying methods of service of process, the City served process on Freddie by publishing notice of the suit in the Monroesville Times for three consecutive weeks. The City did not attempt personal or mail service as not required by the statute. Freddie saw the notice in the Times but did not respond. Assume Freddie does nothing to respond to the suit and the City gets a judgment on the tax lien.

1. What is Freddie's **best** legal argument to challenge the judgment?

   a. Freddie should argue the state statute is constitutionally invalid under the 14th Amendment Due Process clause.

   b. Freddie should argue the City must serve him in person to comport with the 14th Amendment requirements for due process.

   c. Freddie should argue the City was required to serve him by mail or personal service.

   d. Freddie should argue that constructive notice alone was constitutionally inadequate when the City could ascertain his whereabouts.

2. What is the City's **best** argument in defense of the judgment?

   a. The City should argue Freddie does not have a protected property interest.

   b. The City should argue constructive notice through publication was adequate because, under these circumstances, the notice was reasonably calculated to apprise Freddie of the action.

   c. The City should argue Freddie is barred from asserting notice was improper when he admits to seeing the notice in the paper.

   d. The City should argue service by publication was constitutionally valid as Freddie's interest in the property was not reasonably ascertainable.

Lindsey Greene was a tenant in a public housing apartment complex leased and managed by Coastal Housing Authority. Lindsey, a 24-year-old mother of three, ran behind on her rent payments. Coastal, acting under the lease provisions, initiated an action for eviction against Lindsey. Coastal filed the eviction action and sent a process server to Lindsey's apartment to serve notice of the suit. While at the apartment, the server noticed children playing in the apartment common areas and halls, and papers and notices torn from bulletin boards and doors throughout the complex. The server knocked on Lindsey's door but she was not at home. The server then posted the notice of the eviction action on Lindsey's door. Coastal did not mail or publish other notice to Lindsey and the server did not make another attempt to serve Lindsey personally.

Sometime during the day, before Lindsey arrived home, the posted notice was torn from her door. She did not know she was the subject of an eviction action until Coastal arrived on her doorstep several weeks later to evict her and her three children under the authority of the Court's eviction judgment.

3. Was Coastal's service by posted notice constitutionally adequate under the standard set in *Mennonite Board of Missions v. Adams*? Select the **best** answer.

   a. Yes, Coastal's service by posting the notice on Lindsey's door was adequate because it was reasonably calculated to apprise Lindsey of the eviction action against her.

   b. No, Coastal's service by posting the notice on Lindsey's door was not adequate because eviction impacts an individual's property interest, therefore personal service is required by the 14th Amendment Due Process clause.

   c. No, if Coastal knew Lindsey's location, they had a duty to provide more than constructive notice and should have used an additional means of serving notice such as mail or in person service.

   d. Yes, Coastal's service by posting the notice on Lindsey's door was adequate because it constituted personal service. Coastal is not responsible for the actions of children or others in the apartment complex that may have removed the notice before Lindsey returned home.

Chapter 4

PROCEDURAL DUE PROCESS

INTRODUCTION

When lawyers initiate litigation and thereby invoke government power to adjudicate a claim, they must use procedures that satisfactorily give notice and an opportunity to be heard to persons and entities they claim remedies against. These foundational due process requirements generally must exist before governments, acting through their courts, can legitimately deprive individuals and entities of property or liberty by awarding and enforcing judicial judgments after decisionmaking by judges and, occasionally, jurors. Requiring notice and an opportunity to be heard sustains the fairness and legitimacy of the American adversarial approach to adjudication.

All of the applicable federal statutes and rules of civil procedure creating and shaping civil litigation in federal courts and state judiciaries, and local rules in these forums, must comport with minimum due process requirements. Virtually all aspects of these existing structural and procedural scaffolds satisfy due process standards so lawyers' civil litigation activities rarely involve applying these constitutional dimensions. Knowledge and skilled use of due process concepts arises only in applications of these existing rules to unique, unusual or extraordinary factual situations, or in novel complex procedural contexts. Most lawyers seldom confront these contexts.

Constitutional provisions guaranteeing due process do not specify exactly what notice should say, how it should be communicated, and what procedural components opportunities for hearings encompass. The broad, general language found in the due process clauses of the 5th and 14th Amendments to the United States Constitution, have generated several opinions by the United States Supreme Court interpreting these provisions. These opinions create flexible, multiple factor, balancing tests for most of the common contexts in which due process concerns and controversies arise. These contexts include giving notice, providing appropriate hearing opportunities, determining whether hearings must occur before temporary judicial action is taken, adjudicating what must be involved in hearings, and providing unfettered access to courts. Other contexts in which procedural due process arise include the appropriate reach of one state's judicial power against non-resident defendants, and the ability to preclude litigants from re-litigating issues decided in earlier disputes when their interests were arguably represented adequately. Applications of rules and concepts in these contexts are discussed in other chapters.

Due process claims are about procedure. The due process constitutional guarantee sets out the elements that lawyers asserting these claims must allege and prove.

These elements include: (1) deprivation; (2) by state actor or private person or entity acting under color of state law; (3) of life, liberty, or property; and (4) without due process of law. Determining the existence of the first three elements is seldom difficult. Persuading courts what due process requires in particular contexts, however, typically presents more challenges. It requires choosing the applicable balancing test, and then demonstrating that factors and policy reasons point in your client's direction.

EXERCISE 1: WHICH PROCESS — WHOSE TV?

FOCUS OF THIS EXERCISE: Comparing adjudicatory and consensual dispute resolution.

SKILLS INVOLVED: Experiencing process level similarities and differences between adjudicatory and consensual dispute resolution in either advocate or third party neutral roles, including different information use, focus, and outcomes.

ESTIMATED TIME FOR COMPLETING THIS EXERCISE:

30 minutes

ESTIMATED LEVEL OF DIFFICULTY: Somewhat easy

EXERCISE 1:   WHICH PROCESS — WHOSE TV?

For this exercise we divide into three person groups. Two members of each group will play the role of roommates who are ending their time sharing space but have a dispute about an antique television that they both want. The third person plays the role of the neutral judge and decision-maker in the first exercise, and a mediator in the second exercise.

The first exercise is a short trial where each roommate has five minutes to make all the arguments they wish in support of their contention that they are entitled to this television. The judge listens to these arguments and may not ask questions of the roommates. The roommates may address only the judge and may not address each other. When both sides are finished, the judge makes a decision privately, writes it down, and does not reveal it.

The next exercise is a short mediation of this same situation. The roommates have a total of fifteen minutes to talk to each other and, with the mediator's help, try to reach an agreement. The mediator may ask questions and suggest resolution possibilities. To save time, mediators should not make an opening statement or use private caucuses. Beyond that, mediators should do whatever they think will help these roommates reach agreement.

After the mediation ends, the judge-mediators announce and explain the decision they made after the trial.

WEBCOURSE FOR EXERCISE 1: Please check the **LexisNexis Webcourse** for additional material that may be posted for this exercise.

EXERCISE 2: PROFILE BOOK BANISHMENT

FOCUS OF THIS EXERCISE: Conduct a client interview to assess suitability of a due process claim.

SKILLS INVOLVED: Identifying and formulating relevant legal theories by applying knowledge of elements of a due process claim and alternative possibilities, and making engaged decisions about what to do and not do when interviewing to communicate effectively and gather information needed to make decisions regarding applying law to solve client problems.

ESTIMATED TIME FOR COMPLETING THIS EXERCISE:

45 minutes

ESTIMATED LEVEL OF DIFFICULTY: Moderate

YOUR ROLE IN THIS EXERCISE: Play either the lawyer or client and prepare for and then conduct a short interview directed toward gathering information to determine whether a valid due process claim exists in this situation.

WEBCOURSE FOR EXERCISE 2: Please check the **LexisNexis Webcourse** for additional material that may be posted for this exercise.

Memorandum
To: General Intake File
From: Abbie Allen, paralegal

Re: Intake phone interview

This morning I briefly interviewed [assume an appropriate name as clients will be using their actual names, and s/he will be identified here by the impersonal phrase "the client," and awkward s/he and his/her phrasings]. The client has a complaint against Profile Book. The client said s/he was an active and regular user of Profile Book until last week when s/he was suddenly and inexplicably banished from the site.

This involved a Web 2.0 application. The client said s/he invested a lot of time creating profiles and uploading information on his/her Profile Book profile. S/he said the profile was used to communicate with people, and gather information for use in his/her blogging. S/he works part-time as a paid blogger for a local site and uses this income to supplement his/her undergraduate education at the local university. The client was concerned that this could impact his/her job, as well as his/her friendships and professional relationships. S/he also indicated that s/he had received emails from several friends who wondered where s/he had gone. Some indicated they thought s/he might be ignoring them, or might no longer be their Profile Book friend.

With the client's help, I checked Profile Book's website which has a FAQ about disabled accounts. I pasted what it says here:

> Your account was disabled because you violated Profile Book's Term's of Use, which you agreed to when you first registered for an account on this site. Accounts can either be disabled for repeat offenses or for one, particularly egregious violation.

> Profile Book does not allow users to register with fake names, or impersonate any person or entity, or to falsely state or otherwise misrepresent themselves or their affiliations.

> We do not allow users to send unsolicited or harassing messages to people they don't know, and we remove posts that advertise a product, service, website, or opportunity.

> Our Code of Conduct outlines the types of content we do not allow on the site. This includes any obscene, pornographic, or sexually explicit photos, as well as any photos that depict graphic violence. We also remove content, photographic or written, that threatens, intimidates, harasses, or brings unwanted attention or embarrassment to an individual or group of people.

The client insisted that s/he did not do anything of these things. S/he wanted to see the allegedly offending content that caused the banishment. S/he indicated that the applicable FAQ was perhaps inspired by Kranz Kafka because it says:

> Unfortunately, for technical and security reasons, Profile Book cannot provide you with a description or copy of the removed content.

The client wants to know what his/her legal rights are. I explained that I would submit this summary to our normal intake procedure and one of our lawyers would contact him/her soon to discuss the matter.

Chapter 5

THE *ERIE* DOCTRINE OF CHOICE OF LAW

INTRODUCTION

Now that you have tackled the difficult constitutional topics of jurisdiction and procedural due process, you may be asked to consider the vexing *Erie* doctrine. When you are first introduced to this topic and the doctrine's namesake case, *Erie Railroad Co. v. Tompkins*,[1] you will most likely find the reading in your casebook complex. Despite all contrary appearances, the first step in tackling the *Erie* doctrine is understanding that the doctrine itself is not complicated. Two key things make the *Erie* doctrine difficult for first year law students in Civil Procedure to understand: (1) the historical context of the *Erie* case and the concept of general common law, and (2) the application of the doctrine to modern diversity cases.

The Story Before *Erie*

To understand the *Erie* case, you must place the case in context. Like so many cases in the constitutional portion of your Civil Procedure course, the real import lies in what comes before. In the matter of *Erie*, the real case at issue is *Swift v. Tyson*.[2] The United States Supreme Court decided the *Swift* case in 1842, and its ruling stood for 96 years, until *Erie* came along. In *Swift*, the Supreme Court decided that federal courts sitting in diversity did not have to apply state law to all aspects of a diversity case. Under the *Swift* doctrine, federal courts sitting in diversity could apply federal general common law to the substantive legal issues in the case.

The issue of what law to apply to a case in federal court based on diversity jurisdiction is the heart of the *Erie* doctrine. As we discussed in Chapter Two, cases reach federal court via two main routes of subject matter jurisdiction: federal question jurisdiction and jurisdiction based on diversity of citizenship. However, just because a case has proper subject matter jurisdiction in federal court does not mean federal law is the proper law to be applied to the case. For example, a plaintiff from North Carolina can bring suit against a defendant from New York in federal court on a simple negligence claim (as long as the claim meets the amount in controversy). The case is properly in federal court, but which state's law should apply to resolve the negligence case? This question is unique to diversity cases because cases in federal court under federal question jurisdiction are cases which include a question of federal law. In those cases, federal law applies. However, in diversity cases, the court must decide which law applies to the claim.

---

[1] *Erie Railroad Co. v. Tompkins*, 304 U.S. 64 (1908).

[2] *Swift v. Tyson*, 41 U.S. 1 (1842).

The Supreme Court in *Swift* interpreted section 34 of the Judiciary Act of 1789 (codified as 28 U.S.C. § 1652) to provide that federal courts sitting in diversity did not have to apply state common law. The *Swift* court found that if the legal issue in the diversity case was controlled by a state statute or other codified law, the federal court had to apply that state law to the diversity case. But, according to *Swift*, that rule did not apply if the law at issue was judge-made, what we commonly refer to as the common law. In fact, the *Swift* Court allowed for the creation of a federal general common law that could be invoked by federal judges in diversity cases when the only state law applicable to the case was judge-made common law. Although the concept of a federal general common law sounded good to many, the reality was that the *Swift* decision led to abuse, unfairness, and forum shopping. If a party could avoid its state law by filing the case in federal court under the diversity statute, then it may even go as far as to move or change its corporate citizenship to create diversity and take advantage of a more favorable federal general common law.[3]

So why is this important to understanding the *Erie* doctrine? Principally because the *Erie* case overruled *Swift* and held that there was no federal general common law. *Erie* rejected the narrow interpretation of section 34 and ruled that when a diversity case involved state common law, that state's common law would be applied. Although the Court's decision in *Erie* was not beneficial to Mr. Tompkins, the Plaintiff, who was a trespasser under Pennsylvania law, the decision did render a more consistent, predictable, and fair template for the choice of law in diversity cases.

The rule of *Erie* is often generally stated as follows: when a case is in federal court based on diversity of citizenship, the federal court applies federal procedural law and state substantive law. The *Erie* case does not actually use the language of "procedural" and "substantive" in this context (although Justice Reed's concurring opinion comes close), but this construct of procedural vs. substantive law is what we commonly refer to as the *Erie* doctrine.

Applying *Erie*

Now that we have identified the doctrine and explored why the case itself is treated with such importance, we move on to what proves to be the most difficult part; understanding the procedural/substantive dichotomy. In many cases, the application of the doctrine is so obvious it does not merit mention by the court or the parties. At this point, it is understood that the Federal Rules of Civil Procedure (created in 1938, the same year of the *Erie* decision) are the procedural rules in federal court. Thus, when a party in federal court challenges the content of the pleadings, the federal court will apply the Federal Rules of Civil Procedure to resolve the controversy. The *Erie* question arises when the line between procedural law and substantive law is not so clear-cut. For example, is the relevant statute of limitations a procedural or substantive law? Is an evidentiary rule which prohibits the introduction of evidence of out of court settlements in joint tortfeasor cases a procedural or substantive law? These questions, like many others, are decided by the federal courts on a case-by-case basis; however, there is an analytical template for resolving an *Erie* question which

---

[3] *See Black and White Taxicab and Transfer Co. v. Brown*, 276 U.S. 518 (1928).

can lead you to a strong argument for either side.

EXERCISE 1: SUBSTANTIVE vs. PROCEDURAL:
THE STATUTE OF LIMITATIONS

FOCUS OF THIS EXERCISE: This exercise is designed to allow you to practice analyzing a choice of law question under the *Erie* doctrine. In this exercise, you should focus on the substantive/procedural dichotomy that followed *Erie* and consider whether the relevant party action invokes procedural or substantive law implications.

SKILLS INVOLVED: Legal analysis; creating an answer to a hypothetical for purposes of an oral discussion with a judge.

ESTIMATED TIME FOR COMPLETING THE EXERCISE: 30 minutes

ESTIMATED LEVEL OF DIFFICULTY: Moderate

YOUR ROLE IN THIS EXERCISE: In this exercise, you should act and think in the role of a judicial clerk, advising a judge on how to rule on a motion. When analyzing the fact scenario below, imagine that the judge has asked you to review this question over lunch and wants to meet with you after lunch to discuss your analysis. You should be prepared to offer a conversational analysis of the issue.

EXERCISE 1:   SUBSTANTIVE vs. PROCEDURAL: THE STATUTE OF LIMITATIONS

Factual Scenario: A Virginia state statute dictates that any negligence action must be brought within three years of the date of the negligent act. Under Virginia state law, the statute of limitations is not tolled, thus does not stop running, until the lawsuit is served on the defendant (as contrasted with other state laws which toll the statute of limitations when the complaint is filed, not served).

On May 1, yr-4,[4] Chris, a pedestrian, was slammed into by an errant bicyclist, Phil, and suffered leg and back injuries as a result. Chris was a citizen of Virginia. Phil was from New York. On April 30, yr-1, Chris filed a complaint naming Phil as the defendant alleging damages in excess of $100,000. Wishing to avoid the Virginia statute of limitations which is tolled at service, not filing, Chris filed his case in the Federal District Court for the Eastern District of Virginia because federal court pleading rules provide that the statute is tolled when the complaint is filed at the court house, not when it is served. Phil moves to dismiss the lawsuit under Rule 12(b)(6), alleging that Virginia law applies to the question of whether Chris's lawsuit was filed within the applicable statute of limitations and that the three year period had expired because Chris did not serve his lawsuit on Phil within three years. According to Virginia law, the applicable statute of limitations had run by the time Phil was served on June 20, yr-1. Chris argues that the question of whether the statute of limitations is tolled at the filing of the complaint or service of the complaint is a question of procedural law, thus controlled by the Federal Rules, not Virginia Law.

Assume you are a judicial clerk assigned to the Federal District Court Judge assigned to the case. The Judge has asked you to be prepared to discuss the action that should be taken on the Motion. Using the analysis of *Erie* and its progeny, analyze whether the Federal District Court should grant Phil's motion. Summaries of some relevant cases are provided below.

---

[4] yr-4 indicates that the year dated is four years ago from the current date. For example if you are working on this exercise in 2014, the accident occurred on May 1, 2010.

CASE SUMMARY:
RAGAN v. MERCHANTS TRANSFER & WAREHOUSE CO.
337 U.S. 530 (1949)

This case was originally brought in Kansas Federal District Court on the basis of diversity of citizenship. The Petitioner was involved in a highway accident on October 1, 1943 and filed a complaint, invoking diversity jurisdiction, with the Federal District Court on September 4, 1945. The summons was subsequently served on Respondent on December 28, 1945, after the expiration of the Kansas two-year statute of limitations. Respondent argued that the two-year statute of limitations had run because, under Kansas law, the statute was not tolled until service of the summons, thus the lawsuit was commenced after the expiration of the statute of limitations. Petitioner relied on Federal Rule of Civil Procedure 3 which deemed a civil action commenced at the time the complaint was filed, not served. Thus, according to Petitioner, the filing of the complaint tolled the statute.

The District Court held in favor of the Petitioner on this point, the Court of Appeals reversed, and the case was appealed to the United States Supreme Court. The Supreme Court held that state laws governing the applicable statute of limitations were substantive not procedural. As to which rule controlled the tolling of the statute, the Court further stated they could not give the statute of limitations a longer life in the federal court than it would have in the state court without adding something to the cause of action, which would require judicial action inconsistent with *Erie*. The Court held that allowing plaintiffs able to invoke diversity in federal courts a longer statute of limitations for their claims would encourage forum shopping and defeat the goals of *Erie*.

See also Woods v. Interstate Realty Co., 337 U.S. 535 (1949), and *Cohen v. Beneficial Industrial Loan Corp.*, 337 U.S. 541 (1949).

CASE SUMMARY:
HANNA v. PLUMER
380 U.S. 460 (1965)

This case was originally brought in Massachusetts Federal District Court on the basis of diversity of citizenship. The plaintiff filed a complaint claiming damages for personal injuries sustained in an automobile accident in South Carolina. The plaintiff alleged claims of negligence in her complaint against defendant, who was a Massachusetts citizen. The plaintiff complied with Rule 4 of the Federal Rules of Civil Procedure when she served defendant by leaving a copy of the summons and complaint with defendant's wife at his residence. When defendant filed his answer, he sought dismissal arguing the action could not be maintained because service of process did not comply with the Massachusetts rule for service of process.

The Federal District Court granted defendant's motion holding that the Massachusetts rule controlled. The Court of Appeals affirmed the decision, and the plaintiff appealed the case to the United States Supreme Court on the question of whether service of process is a "procedural" or "substantive" question under *Erie*. The Supreme Court reversed the lower court, finding that service of process in a diversity action filed in Federal District Court is a procedural matter and controlled by the Federal Rules of Civil Procedure, even when those rules conflict with the state rules. The Court held, "[t]o hold that a Federal Rule of Civil Procedure must cease to function whenever it alters the mode of enforcing state-created rights would be to disembowel either the Constitution's grant of power over federal procedure or Congress's attempt to exercise that power in the [Rules] Enabling Act."

Webcourse for Exercise 1:

Access the *Erie* Doctrine Analysis Flow Chart on the **LexisNexis Webcourse** that was created for this book and use it to organize your analysis of the exercise. You may also want to access the Review Podcast on *Erie* which is also available on the **LexisNexis Webcourse** that was created for this book.

EXERCISE 2: SUBSTANTIVE vs. PROCEDURAL: ADMISSIBLE EVIDENCE

FOCUS OF THIS EXERCISE: This exercise is designed to allow you to practice analyzing questions under the *Erie* doctrine. In this exercise, you should focus on the substantive/procedural dichotomy that followed *Erie* and consider whether the relevant party action invokes procedural or substantive law implications.

SKILLS INVOLVED: Legal analysis through understanding case law and applying the relevant rules to a new fact situation.

ESTIMATED TIME FOR COMPLETING THE EXERCISE:

30 to 45 minutes

ESTIMATED LEVEL OF DIFFICULTY: Moderate

YOUR ROLE IN THIS EXERCISE: You are playing the role of a law clerk in this exercise and are preparing to discuss a case with the judge. Your goal is to think through the problem and develop a set of notes that will allow you to brief the judge on the relevant issues and analysis in an oral conversation. You should also practice talking through the analysis so you will be prepared for the discussion in the meeting.

EXERCISE 2:   SUBSTANTIVE vs. PROCEDURAL: ADMISSIBLE EVIDENCE

Factual Scenario: Jennifer brings a negligence action against Chris in Tennessee Federal District Court claiming diversity jurisdiction. As the parties prepare the case for trial, Jennifer plans to call a witness to discuss Chris's psychiatric history, which has been determined relevant to her case against Chris. Under Tennessee rules, an examining physician may publish copies of Chris's psychiatric records to the jury if that information is otherwise admissible at trial. However, Federal Rule of Evidence 308(b)(2)(A) provides that the psychiatric records cannot be published to the jury. At trial, the Judge follows the Tennessee law and allows Jennifer to publish Chris's records to the jury. Chris appeals the Judge's action as an error at trial, arguing that the Federal District Court should have followed the Federal rule, not the Tennessee rule, when determining whether to allow the records to be published. On appeal to the Federal Circuit Court, Jennifer argues the Tennessee rule is substantive and thus, under the *Erie* doctrine, was correctly applied in her diversity case. Chris's brief argues that the issue is an evidentiary issue, thus clearly a procedural issue which should be governed by the Federal Rules of Evidence.

You are a judicial clerk for the Judge on the appellate panel who will be authoring the opinion. You should review *Erie* and other relevant case law to determine whether this case should be affirmed or reversed on appeal. You should also review the *Carota* case (case summary below). Your Judge wants to talk through the issue at a meeting before beginning a draft opinion.

CASE SUMMARY:
CAROTA v. JOHNS MANVILLE CORP.
893 F.2d 448 (1st Cir. 1990).

After a trial in Massachusetts Federal District Court on Plaintiff's claim against Celotex for the death of her husband, the Plaintiff, Mrs. Carota, appealed the District Court's ruling on an evidentiary issue to the First Circuit Court of Appeals. On appeal, Plaintiff argued that Defendant Celotex should not have been allowed to introduce evidence of Plaintiff's out-of-court settlements with other parties in a joint tortfeasor case, relying on Federal Rule of Evidence 408 which prohibits the introduction of this evidence at trial. Defendant responded that Massachusetts law does not prohibit the introduction of evidence of other settlements and allows the jury to consider out-of-court settlements when determining a damages award to the plaintiff. The First Circuit Court of Appeals acknowledged that rules governing evidence are procedural, but the law of damages has been determined substantive since damages law determines what award will be received from the case. The court also acknowledged that evidentiary rules regarding out-of-court settlement evidence arguably fall within the zone of substance and procedure. However, the court held that when a state permits the admission of out-of-court settlement evidence with the intent that this evidence may affect the damage award, the issue must be deemed substantive. Accordingly, the Circuit Court upheld the District Court's decision that Massachusetts's law should have been followed and Federal Rule of Evidence 408 did not apply.

See also Sibbach v. Wilson & Company, 312 U.S. 1 (1941); *Gasperini v. Center for Humanities, Inc.,* 518 U.S. 415 (1996).

Webcourse for Exercise 2:

Access the *Erie* Doctrine Analysis Chart on the **LexisNexis Webcourse** that was created for this book and use it to organize your analysis of the exercise. You may also want to access the Review Podcast on *Erie* which is also available on the **LexisNexis Webcourse** that was created for this book.

Chapter 6

VENUE

INTRODUCTION

Venue regulates the geographic location of where lawsuits are filed and tried. All court systems have geographic units. The federal court system consists of 94 judicial districts with every state having at least one and some as many as four. State court systems sometimes describe their geographic units differently using labels such as counties and circuits. Venue provisions are typically articulated in statutes or procedural rules. They often encompass general provisions applied broadly and special provisions dealing with specific claims.

Venue provisions authorize which courts within a chosen court system lawsuits should be filed. They typically present acceptable options such as the geographic judicial units where defendants reside or claims arose. Venue provisions emphasize convenience to litigants, witnesses, and courts. They generally assume that where defendants reside is convenient, and where claims arose is fair because this locale usually encompasses where witnesses and evidence exist.

Lawyers apply knowledge of applicable venue provisions and strategic and planning skills when considering this part of the choice regarding where to file a claim, or whether they can and should object to the plaintiff's geographic choice. The plaintiff's first goal typically is to ensure that they choose an appropriate location so that defendants cannot affect their choice by either getting the lawsuit dismissed or transferred to a more appropriate venue. Although general federal venue provisions authorize courts to dismiss cases filed in the wrong venue, they also suggest that transferring cases to proper districts should be done in the interests of justice. [28 USC 1406(a)] The common law doctrine of *forum non conveniens* usually generates dismissals but it now exercises practical importance primarily in international and state litigation.

Exercising strategic and planning skills, lawyers assess a range of factors in choosing between appropriate venue options for their lawsuits. These factors include practical considerations such as convenience and costs via travel and work disruption for plaintiffs, their lawyers, and principal witnesses. Legal factors include assessing substantive law differences regarding statutes of limitations, claim elements, allowable damages, and the reach of subpoena powers over potentially uncooperative but important witnesses. Finally, lawyers assess important tactical factors including influencing the choice of judges, the desirability of prospective jury pools, and current docket conditions when choosing between appropriate venues.

Our adversarial system gives defendants abilities to seek to transfer venue from appropriate forums to other appropriate locales that are arguably more convenient. [e.g., 28 U.S.C. § 1404] Courts assess many of the above factors when ruling on these motions. They often accord significant deference to a plaintiff's venue choice, and often reduce this when plaintiffs neither reside nor have significant contact with their chosen forum. Many decisions also suggest that less deference is due when blatant forum shopping exists. Substantive law of the original choice follows transfers to discourage defendants' from forum shopping in diversity matters.

Because venue provisions are designed in part to protect defendants from being forced to litigate in unfair forums, defendants can waive these protections by failing to raise improper venue in a Federal Rule 12 motion or their answer. It follows that parties are free to agree where cases may be filed before litigation, typically in a venue or forum selection clause in a contract. These provisions are typically upheld as long as they do not result from fraud or overreaching and the selected venue is not unreasonable or unjust. This makes them an increasingly important part of contract negotiations.

EXERCISE 1: ONCE UPON APOD

FOCUS OF THIS EXERCISE: Negotiating a venue selection clause.

SKILLS INVOLVED: Understanding venue rules and negotiating a venue selection clause.

ESTIMATED TIME FOR COMPLETING THIS EXERCISE:

45 minutes

ESTIMATED LEVEL OF DIFFICULTY: Moderate

YOUR ROLE IN THIS EXERCISE: You will play the role of a lawyer representing either APOD, Inc., a franchisor, or a lawyer negotiating for a franchise, and concentrate your negotiation on a proposed venue selection clause.

WEBCOURSE FOR EXERCISE 1: Please check the **LexisNexis Webcourse** for additional material that may be posted for this exercise.

EXERCISE 1:   ONCE UPON APOD

Venue Negotiation

APOD, Inc. [AI] is this country's fastest growing company in the expanding personal storage industry. AI developed and marketed the concept of providing pods to businesses and homeowners. AI supplies metal pods that business and home owners pack with office or home furniture, files, and other materials, and then transfers them to secure, air-conditioned storage areas. AI is incorporated and headquartered in Wellington, the largest city in West Dakota.

AI runs 100% of its business through a franchise operation. It licenses franchisees to use its trademarks, operating systems, national advertising, and pods. It provides franchisees with market research data, advertising assistance, ongoing training in storage management, and guidance in accounting, cost management, and inventory control. Its approach allows franchisees to enter the storage business with minimum entry barriers and enhanced chances for success. Gaining an AI franchise requires an initial $100,000 franchise fee and a monthly payment of royalties computed at 7% of gross sales. AI also typically imposes requirements concerning advertising, sales and promotions fees, and compliance with strict standards regarding packing and maintenance of pods.

In the interest of time, this negotiation will focus on only one provision of a much longer franchise contract. This provision is a venue selection clause that reads:

"All signors to this document agree that any claim or dispute between them arising out of, or in any way related to, this Agreement, shall be, at the option of the franchisor, either arbitrated in the Southern District of West Dakota, or litigated in the Northern District of West Dakota."

Wellington is located in the Southern District of West Dakota, and the city where the United States District Court for the Northern District of West Dakota is located is 150 miles away. The Northern District of West Dakota has achieved a statistically demonstrable reputation as housing juries that are particularly pro-defendant in resolving claims brought against businesses located in West Dakota.

Chapter 7

PLEADING

INTRODUCTION

Lawyers engage in strategic decision-making about pleading once choices are made to invoke litigation to accomplish client objectives. Pleadings are documents that encompass claims made on behalf of clients against other persons, entities, and governmental units, and defenses raised by those claimed against. Traditionally written but now increasingly electronic, pleadings also articulate defenses and other responses made in response to complaints asserted.

America's adversarial approach to adjudication ensures that most lawyers make pleading decisions from perspectives of clients seeking to assert claims and clients seeking to defend lawsuits filed against them. When doing this, they typically interpret and apply provisions of eleven important Federal Rules of Civil Procedure. The simple language contained in these provisions provides ample opportunities to develop and contest differing interpretations in adversarial interactions. They often create collateral procedural skirmishes that pursue negotiation and other goals that are not focused on adjudicating the facts and legal merits contained in the claims and defenses asserted in pleadings.

Most fundamental principles of pleading analysis and drafting apply equally to whether lawyers are representing parties seeking or defending claims for judicial remedies. Pleadings that begin lawsuits, typically called complaints, start time clocks that regulate many pre-trial procedures. They also usually stop the running of statutes of limitations, time periods within which claims must be asserted under penalty of forfeiture. Lawyers drafting complaints near the expiration of limitation periods must exercise particular care because changes through later amendments must satisfy stringent relation back standards.

Absent urgent demands of quickly approaching statutes of limitations, pleadings seeking initial affirmative relief should reflect extensive factual and legal research to map the most effective routes to accomplishing client objectives. This investigation and research must meet relatively high standards. These standards require that factual contentions either have evidentiary support or be likely to have such after a reasonable opportunity for further investigation and discovery. Claims asserted must be either warranted by existing law or by nonfrivolous arguments to extend, modify, or reverse existing law or to establish new law.

American law makes plaintiffs masters of their complaints, meaning that they choose the claims they wish their lawsuit to assert and the parties they elect to sue, the court in which to litigate and, if permitted, whether to request a jury or rely on a judge to adjudicate their contentions. This strategic planning incorporates considerations of claim elements, proof requirements, abilities to provide sufficient evidence, and potentially different statutes of limitations. Applying concepts covered elsewhere, it measures whom to sue incorporating concerns about relief needed, accomplishing service of process, preventing removal from state to federal courts and venue transfers within court systems, abilities to satisfy judgments, and potentially different discovery standards available from parties and non-parties. Anticipating other considerations presented elsewhere, this strategic planning also makes the initial choice about which court's judicial power to invoke, choosing between state and federal tribunals, and among courts located in different geographical locales within each system.

Because pleading occurs in an adversarial framework, complaint drafters must consider and seek to counter challenges adversaries are likely to make. For example, drafting claims for relief requires application of strategic thinking to ensure accurate compliance with provisions of FRCP 8(a). These provisions require a short and plain statement of the court's jurisdiction grounds, and the pleader's entitlement to relief. Showing entitlement to relief adequately requires the most challenging strategic analysis because United States Supreme Court opinions have held that this short, ambiguous phrase encompasses two facets.

Little controversy exists regarding the facet which permits measuring the legal validity of the claim's basis at this initial stage of a lawsuit. Raised by a motion to dismiss for failure to state a claim upon which can be granted, this challenge questions the substantive law premises upon which claims rest. If courts decide that substantive law allows these claims, lawsuits proceed. If not, however, courts dismiss them and permit no amendment. This leaves appealing the legal decision the trial court made as the only remaining option. Motions to strike that challenge the sufficiency of asserted defenses raise similar challenges of legal validity.

The second and murkier facet of relief entitlement arises when 12(b)(6) challenges do not contest the legal validity of the substantive law premises underlying claims. Analysis of these challenges necessarily focuses on facts instead of underlying legal theories. This analysis predicts how courts prioritize whether litigants must plead facts sufficient only to give notice of claims asserted, or whether they must allege something more to permit some screening of factually deficient claims at this early stage. For many years, the United States Supreme Court's *Conley v. Gibson* opinion emphasized the notice function, and opined that all that is required is notice of a viable claim. This and subsequent opinions de-emphasized assessing pleadings to determine whether claims allege adequate facts to eliminate potentially deficient claims. The United States Supreme Court's 2007 opinion in *Bell Atlantic Corp. v. Twombly* apparently changed this approach by requiring alleging facts sufficient to raise reasonable expectations that discovery will demonstrate a sufficient claim. Numerous unanswered questions regarding applying *Bell Atlantic's* rule and rationale has re-injected substantial uncertainty into compliance with this facet of relief entitlement and increased the level of adversarial skirmishing about it.

Lawyers navigating what relief entitlement means in adversarial pleading must carefully assess context factors relating to claims they choose to assert. If the underlying legal premises of claims are well established, little risk of legal invalidity exist and analysis turns to what facts need to be alleged. If not, lawyers often allege virtually all potentially persuasive facts that they believe they can prove notwithstanding Rule 8(a)'s admonition in to allege short and plain statements because complaints supply the primary appellate record in the event a dismissal is granted. When assessing factual allegations, lawyers may need to allege more specific facts that were formerly needed. This may be particularly true for claims where specific information may be hard to acquire without discovery, and conclusory allegations may trigger a *Bell Atlantic* concern that forcing defendants to endure discovery when nothing is alleged that raises a reasonable expectation of sufficiency is not fair. This includes commonly litigated claims based on alleged discrimination, civil rights violations, conspiracy [the antitrust context involved in *Bell Atlantic*], and similar legal remedies based on facts relatively easy to allege and challenging to prove.

Lawyers responding to claims asserted against their client must apply similarly strategic and predictive thinking on these three levels: (1) challenging procedural aspects of lawsuits; (2) responding to factual allegations; and (3) alleging defenses and additional claims against the parties suing them, co-defendants, and others who may be liable to them in the event they are found liable to plaintiffs. Rule 12 allows responsive pleaders to make early challenges to plaintiff-made decisions regarding the court selected by objecting to subject matter jurisdiction, personal jurisdiction, and venue, all topics covered elsewhere. The same rule permits raising preliminary procedural challenges to the sufficiency of process, and its service. All of these challenges, including questions about the legal validity of claims and the choices made alleging them factually, postpone the time for filing pleadings that respond to the allegations made in the complaint.

Drafting responsive pleadings requires careful strategic thinking about admitting, denying, or asserting lack of sufficient knowledge or information. Denials must be either warranted on evidence or reasonably based on belief or information. In addition to responding to allegations, answers must assert affirmative defenses in short and plain terms. Doing this typically assumes the burden of proving the elements of these defenses, and failing to do this often waives opportunities to rely on these legal theories.

Careful lawyers resist relying on form documents used in other similar cases even though they supply useful guides for accomplishing specific objectives presented by their immediate clients. They know that pleadings frame the discovery, summary judgment, and pre-trial conferencing phases of the journey to trial. They also know that while this framing occurs with the adversarial process, these frames and stages loom large in the negotiations and mediations that often resolve disputes before trial.

EXERCISE 1: SWELTERING PALMS [DECIDING TO SUE]

FOCUS OF THIS EXERCISE: Emphasizing the procedural components, counsel a client regarding whether to file a lawsuit, wait to defend an anticipated lawsuit, or seek to negotiate or mediate the underlying dispute.

SKILLS INVOLVED: Applying and translating legal analysis into clear communication that informs a client and helps him/her make decisions, by identifying and explaining the complex calculus of factors to evaluate before choosing to litigate, including economic costs, time factors, and consensual alternatives.

ESTIMATED TIME FOR COMPLETING THIS EXERCISE: 60 to 90 minutes

ESTIMATED LEVEL OF DIFFICULTY: Somewhat difficult

YOUR ROLE IN THIS EXERCISE: Play either the lawyer or client and conduct a brief counseling decision to help the client decide which procedural option to choose in a landlord-tenant dispute.

WEBCOURSE FOR EXERCISE 1: Please check the **LexisNexis Webcourse** for additional material that may be posted for this exercise.

EXERCISE 1: SWELTERING PALMS

Lawyer's Information

You recently passed the Columbia Bar Examination and have started working as a staff attorney with the Student Legal Services Program at the University of Columbia. The vast majority of students enrolled at the University are tenants renting residences. Consequently, helping tenants solve legal problems with their landlords is one of the most common services your new employer provides.

Yesterday you interviewed Alex [last name will be actual last name of your colleague playing this role], a first year law student at Columbia University's highly ranked state law school. Alex has a residential tenant problem. You wrote the following fact memo for the case file opened as result of this interview.

"Six months ago Alex rented a one bedroom apartment at Sweltering Palms, one of the many nondescript small apartment complexes near the University. Alex signed a 12 month lease. The day before this interview, Alex got a written document from Jayne Phonda, the manager of Sweltering Palms apartments. This document was entitled "Notice of lease termination and direction to vacate."

This document purported to cancel Alex's written 12 month lease, and it stated: "Pursuant to Section 83.56 of the Columbia Statues, you are hereby notified that your rental agreement at Sweltering Palms is terminated, and this termination is effective immediately." This document gave this explanation "This action is taken because of your failure to comply with Section 83.52 of the Columbia Statutes." In addition, this document gave Alex seven days to vacate, stating: "You shall have 7 days from the date of this notice to vacate the premises," and contained the following language: "If you do not vacate your apartment within seven days of the date herein, appropriate legal eviction proceedings will be commenced."

Alex was convinced that his/her lease was canceled because of his/her environmental activities. Alex has been very active in local environmental work during his/her five undergraduate years at the University of Columbia. Currently Alex is actively engaged in trying to stop the building of a huge apartment complex on land adjacent to Paynes Prairie, a state wildlife preserve just south of University City. Alex contends that this development will imperil several acres of wetlands and might impede the migration of rare Sand Hill cranes that usually spend a few winter months in this preserve.

The University City Daily News just published a letter to the editor that Alex wrote objecting to this development and demanding that the County Commission not issue building permits. Alex also posted mimeographed announcements regarding a meeting of concerned citizens around the university campus, including at several prominent locations in his/her apartment complex. These flyers contained Alex's name, phone number, and residential address.

Although Alex did not receive permission from the Sweltering Palms Management to do this, s/he said this kind of posting apparently often occurs for local bands, concerts, and the like. Alex indicated that nothing in the boiler plate language of his/her nine-page lease specifically prohibits posting meeting notices.

Sweltering Palms is owned by Theodore Turner, one of University City's most active land developers, and a person with whom your office has often tangled. Your supervising attorney said that Turner is the "worst slumlord in town." Alex learned just last week that Turner is the principal member of the development project that he is protesting. According to Alex, a local environmental lawyer [whose name Alex could not remember] said that the developers have already invested $350,000 in this project on top of the cost of the land, and the land price was reported in the newspaper as being "several million dollars." This lawyer also told Alex that the developers have obtained the rezoning they need for this project so the building permits remain their last hurdle, and that the developers are likely to "play hardball" with anyone attempting to stop this venture.

Alex said s/he has already paid his rent on time, and that it is not due again until the beginning of next month. Alex has never done any damage to the apartment. Alex has never had any hassles with Phonda, Sweltering Palms' Manager, or with anyone else holding official positions at the complex. Alex said that no one has ever asked to inspect his/her apartment, and this apartment has never been entered without his/her permission. Alex further said that his/her lease says nothing that relates to this current situation.

Section 83.52 of the Columbia Statutes specifies tenant obligations to maintain the dwelling unit. I carefully went over every subsection with Alex and the only one which could possibly apply is subsection (7). This subsection requires that a tenant: "conduct himself or herself, and require other persons on the premises with his or her consent to conduct themselves, in a manner that does not unreasonably disturb the tenant's neighbors or constitute a breach of the peace."

Alex has a high end component stereo system in this one-bedroom apartment, a rig that s/he conceded was "really too large for the space." Alex likes to listen to music, primarily rap and hip hop, at a loud volume. Alex acknowledged two complaints about loud music from next door neighbors, Walt Steele and Rod Metal. Both are [as Alex termed it] "uptight engineering students." Both complaints occurred on Saturday nights, around midnight, when Alex had finished reading assignments for the upcoming week. Immediately after receiving each complaint, Alex turned the volume down even though, as Alex said, "midnight on Saturday is not late for students." Alex has not received any other complaints or comments about his music from anyone at Sweltering Palms. No management team members or other tenants have ever mentioned it.

Alex believes s/he has "a reasonably good relationship" with Walt and Rod. They are "friendly, but not social," and "they never go out." Alex has no knowledge of either Walt or Rod complaining about the music to Phonda, other members of the management team, or anyone else at Sweltering Palms. Alex thinks this is highly unlikely since Walt and Rod are "so introverted," and no one likes Phonda or management.

Yesterday, Alex had a short, angry conversation with Phonda after getting this termination notice. Alex asked her what was going on, and Phonda responded, "I don't know. This just came from the boss. He didn't explain it to me." When Alex asked who the boss was, Phonda replied "Theodore Turner." Alex then tried to call Turner but got no answer. The message Alex left on Turner's machine has not been returned. Alex has never met Turner or received any form of written communication with him.

Alex wanted to know his/her legal rights, and kept insisting that his/her free speech rights had been infringed. I told Alex I would do some research, talk to my supervising attorney, and get back in no later than three days."

After reviewing the above memo, read the following Memorandum from your Senior Attorney. Then conduct a conference with Alex to help decide what to do next. This process of helping clients make decisions has been frequently called legal counseling. A client-centered approach to this process suggests that lawyers should inform clients fully by helping them identify all reasonable alternatives available to accomplish their objectives. Once options have been identified, lawyers should help their clients identify and evaluate all realistic consequences of each alternative, and then make a decision. Lawyers should ensure that clients identify and assess both non-legal [e.g. social, psychological, and moral] as well as legal [procedural, economic, and likely outcome] consequences. A client-centered approach to counseling also generally encourages lawyers to let their clients to make important decisions and refrain from telling them what to do. This model follows the professional mandate that clients possess "ultimate authority to determine the purposes to be served by legal representation." Comment 1 to Model Rule of Professional Responsibility 1.2.

The Memorandum from your Senior Attorney demonstrates one approach to how that law that could be applied to this decision might be analyzed. Please assume that it accurately reflects all relevant Columbia law and procedure. Your task is to share your knowledge about these alternatives and legal consequences to help Alex decide what to do next.

Memorandum
To: Lawyer handling the Sweltering Palms case
From: Senior Attorney, Student Legal Services

Re: Analysis of Current Situation

I have read your fact memorandum regarding our client's situation at Sweltering Palms. I agree that our client needs to make a decision soon. Bringing the client in for a counseling conference tomorrow makes sense.

The client's options now include: (1) sue now to enjoin the threatened eviction on the basis that it would be an illegal act because it is retaliatory; (2) do nothing now and defend an eviction action if it is filed on the basis of retaliatory conduct and failure to comply with § 83.56(2)(b) of the Columbia Statutes; and (3) seek to negotiate or mediate an acceptable resolution now using both of the previous alternatives as potential leverage. I will briefly analyze each option and list some of their advantages and disadvantages.

A. LEGAL ANALYSIS OF RETALIATORY EVICTION OPTIONS

Our first two options raise a novel legal question of whether a landlord's power over his property should be restricted by preventing evictions which retaliate against tenant conduct unrelated to the rental premises. Research found no appellate opinions in this state dealing with any situation involving these or analogous facts. This memo will survey common law and statutory authority that affect these options.

1. Common Law Authority

The common law evolution of retaliatory eviction in Columbia begins and ends with *Robinson v. Roundtree. Robinson* establishes that Columbia common law will restrict a landlord's freedom to evict if it retaliates against legal tenant conduct. *Robinson* involved an eviction that retaliated against the tenant for her complaint to her landlord about conditions in her apartment. The Court's analysis explicitly linked its recognition of restriction on a landlord's freedom to evict for retaliatory reasons to the policy of promoting the legislative creation of a duty to maintain rental premises in § 83.51 of the Columbia Statutes.

The only portion *of Robinson* that may help us extend its rationale to tenant conduct that doesn't involve a rental unit is its reliance on *Edwards v. Habib*, 397 F.2d 687 (D.C. Cir. 1968), *cert. denied,* 393 U.S. 1016 (1969). *Edwards* was the Federal decision which created the common law defense of retaliatory eviction. It involved a tenant's exercise of constitutionally protected rights to complain to a city housing code enforcement authority about the conditions in her apartment. The *Edwards* opinion emphasized the fact that enforcement of the housing codes depended in part on private initiative in reporting violations. It also expressed concern that permitting retaliatory evictions would punish constitutionally protected activity and inhibit private initiative.

These rationales allow us to use analogous arguments for our client. Our tenant, for example, was exercising constitutionally protected rights to prevent allegedly harmful development next to ecologically sensitive land dedicated to public use. In addition, our ad hoc and heavily bureaucratized approach to environmental protection leaves much to the initiative of private citizens like Alex. Permitting retaliatory eviction to occur here will, as in *Edwards*, punish constitutionally protected activity and inhibit private initiative.

2. Statutory Authority

Section 83.64(1) is the most recent Columbia legal source on the subject of retaliatory conduct. It makes it "unlawful for a landlord to discriminatorily . . . bring or threaten to bring an action for possession . . . primarily because the landlord is retaliating against the tenant." This prohibition is "not limited to" the three types of protected conduct it enumerates. *Id.* In addition, one of these specific examples deals with activities that do not necessarily focus on issues involving any precise rental unit. Section 83.64(1) (b) says that the landlord may not retaliate against a tenant who "has organized, encouraged, or participated in a tenant's organization."

This section could be helpful because organizing, encouraging, or participating in a tenant's organization involves political activity, similar to environmental activism, that may or may not deal with issues affecting specific rental units. Tenant organizations, for example, occasionally exist for purposes other than hassling landlords. We could even argue that our client's conduct in posting meeting announcements containing name, address, and phone number at Sweltering Palms was an attempt to organize a tenant group for environmental purposes.

3. Assessment of These Options

Both our common law and statutory arguments invite rebuttal arguments aimed at limiting retaliatory eviction to situations involving attempts to secure rights regarding specific rental units. The right of property owners to do what they please with their property remains a powerful theme. Values developed in feudal and agrarian times, when land was worked and farmed, still exert strong influence in our contemporary, urban landscape where habitable space, and a broad prohibition against retaliatory conduct, should be predominant concerns.

Predicting whether local judges will buy our arguments is difficult. A suit to enjoin this threatened eviction would have to be filed in circuit court because county courts do not have jurisdiction to grant injunctive relief. We could draw any one of five circuit judges who are currently not assigned to the criminal law docket. All of our circuit judges are white men who range from moderate to narrow in their general judicial temperament. The three younger men are generally moderate and are likely to be receptive to our arguments. I estimate a 65% chance of winning the statutory argument and a 50% change of winning the common law argument if we draw any of these three. The two older men are very narrow in outlook and are not likely to be receptive. They both own rental property. I estimate only a 20% chance of winning either our statutory or common law assertion with these two judges.

Selection of circuit judges is done randomly, by lot, when the case is filed. We can exert no influence over this process. Dismissing and refilling in an attempt to get another judge raises significant ethical problems. Our office does not do this.

If we do not file first and rather wait for Turner to sue, we will be in county court because it has jurisdiction over evictions. The bench there is likely to be more responsive to our argument. We have a random draw between three young judges [two women and one man]. All of them have considerable experience in landlord-tenant law. All have developed a general reputation for being much more willing to listen to novel arguments raised by tenants than previous county judges. Consequently, I estimate our chances with any of the three to be 70% at winning the statutory argument. I put our chances of winning our common law contention at 50% with each of these judges.

A disadvantage of suing first in circuit court is that tenant will have to pay a filing and service of process fee. Those costs are $188.50 for filing and $52 for service. We can shift these costs to Turner if we win. No court costs will have to be paid if we defend the eviction action because Sweltering Palms will have to incur them. They can, however, be shifted to us if we lose. That sum is $129.50.

Another potential disadvantage of both litigation options is the risk of getting stuck with Turner's attorney fees if we lose. Section 83.48 shifts "reasonable attorney's fees" to the "prevailing party" in any landlord-tenant action. Sweltering Palms is represented by Jones & Green, a reputable local firm. They typically bill at $300 an hour. A reasonable estimate of defending our suit or trying their eviction is 12 to 15 hours. All of the judges in front of whom this case might be tried commonly add attorney's fees to the judgment entered against the losing party in landlord-tenant matters. We also run this risk if we choose to wait and defend, the option analyzed next, and lose.

All of our options are vulnerable to losing on facts through a finding that Turner's motivation was not in retaliation for our client's environmental activities but rather because the noise complaints regarding our client's stereo constituted a violation of the lease. I estimate only a 50% probability that we can prevail on this threshold factual question.

We also may lose if Turner can prove a valid basis for the eviction even if we also prove a retaliatory motive. Section 83.64(3) makes our statutory argument inapplicable in a dual motive context. Our common law assertion theoretically could still be made but I doubt that it would be persuasive in this context.

The dual motivation problem probably is our greatest hurdle to winning on a retaliatory eviction theory. It presents such a convenient way for a judge or jury to split the difference between our positions. I therefore predict only a 35% chance that we can convince any of the favorable judges that Turner acted only in retaliation against our client's conduct protesting his Paynes Prairie development. In other words, I think we have a 65% chance of losing on the grounds of dual motivation with favorable judges and an even greater chance of losing this point with unfavorable judges.

An injunction suit would predictably take longer to conclude and thus extend our client's occupancy of the present apartment. I estimate that it will take six to eight weeks to conclude this action following normal procedures set out in the rules. Our client would, however, have to continue paying the rent during this time to avoid being evicted for non-payment.

The eviction, on the other hand, gets accelerated procedural treatment under Columbia law. It should be over in two to three weeks from the date it is filed.

B. OUR OTHER EVICTION DEFENSE

The problems and discovery expense associated with the retaliatory eviction defense can be avoided if our client chooses to assert only his/her statutory defense. Section 83.56(2)(b) requires seven day written notice specifying the tenant's noncompliance and giving an opportunity to correct it if the violation is "of a nature that the tenant should be given an opportunity to cure it." Unfortunately, noise disruption is not listed as one of the enumerated examples of curable violations in this subsection.

Research found no cases dealing with this factual situation, putting us in another ambiguous interpretive situation. Arguably, occasional excess volume on a stereo is as easily curable as are the examples enumerated, such as unauthorized pets, guests, and improper parking. It is also dramatically different from the non-curable violation examples listed in § 83.56(2)(a), such as intentional destruction of property.

Defending on this basis in county court will draw one of those three younger, more tenant-oriented county judges. I estimate an 80% likelihood that we will defeat the eviction with this defense if investigation or discovery confirms that Phonda had not given our client any written warnings. I would put the prediction higher but for the unknown factual possibility that Steele and Metal may have complained to Phonda more than once. This raises a slight risk that a judge could conclude that our client's conduct constituted a "continued unreasonable disturbance" which is not a curable violation under § 83.56(2)(a). Even in this instance, however, Sweltering Palms has to have given our client a "written warning . . . of a similar violation." *Id.*

Winning the eviction on this defense should produce a seven day written notice letting our client cure the violation. If our client cures, no legal [and non-retaliatory] basis will then exist for the eviction.

C. THE NEGOTIATION/MEDIATION OPTION

This approach involves contacting the lawyer at Jones & Green who represents Sweltering Palms and discussing whether a solution can be found that saves everyone time and money. We can suggest either a negotiation or a voluntary mediation.

It is hard to predict whether Jones & Green will agree to talk at this point or, if they do, what the contours of this discussion are likely to be. Both negotiating and mediation is this context is voluntary. As indicated, the two earlier options can be used as leverage. The 83.56(2)(b) defense will probably have the greatest negotiation value because it is the strongest. Our end result might be a written guarantee not to evict our client unless rent goes unpaid or other violations of the lease occur. Perhaps someone at Sweltering Palms would be willing to provide a written apology regarding the anxiety this threatened action has caused.

We also should think about what we can offer Sweltering Palms. Perhaps we should ascertain whether our client would be willing to move out at the end of the lease, [or even before with a sublease] in the event that problems with other tenants that need to be addressed exist. Ideas for providing explicit proof that the stereo problem has been resolved also should be discussed with our client.

D. TORT OPTIONS

If Sweltering Palms goes ahead and evicts our client, he may have a viable tort cause of action for wrongful eviction. Columbia law generally provides that tenants who are wrongfully or unlawfully evicted may bring an action against their landlord for damages. Other torts, such as intentional or negligent interference with a contract relationship, probably don't work since Sweltering Palms is not an outsider to this lease arrangement.

No Columbia cases hold that a retaliatory eviction is an actionable wrongful eviction tort. I did not research this option for several reasons. First, proving that this eviction is unlawful requires establishing that it is retaliatory and that it runs into all the problems summarized earlier.

Second, the amount of damages our client has and will suffer seems fairly slight. Columbia law permits recovering as general damages the actual value or rental value of the unexpired rent term less rent owed. As I understand it, our client's rent may be a bit under market so we could recover the difference. Expenses occurred in renting substitute property and the excess amount of rent paid therewith is also probably recoverable. I'm not sure all of this adds up to much, and the availability of punitive damages has been severely limited by our new tort legislation.

Finally, if this case has significant dollar value, we cannot handle it. As you know, we are obligated to refer cases with significant value to the private bar. Bottom line, I'm not even sure I mention this as an option, but I will leave you that choice.

Good luck with your counseling conference. There is a lot to cover. Let me know how it goes.

EXERCISE 2: JOHN WEBALE v. UNIVERSITY OF WEST DAKOTA [PLEADING PLANNING]

FOCUS OF THIS EXERCISE: Do a brief investigation interview after reviewing case excerpts regarding pleading standards.

SKILLS INVOLVED: First, spotting issues, assimilating and applying precedent, and then gathering information from a supportive colleague.

ESTIMATED TIME FOR COMPLETING THIS EXERCISE:

60 to 90 minutes

ESTIMATED LEVEL OF DIFFICULTY: Difficult

YOUR ROLE IN THIS EXERCISE: You will play the role of either a lawyer representing John Webale who wants to sue his employer, the University of West Dakota, for denying him promotion because of racial discrimination, or a Union Advocate who has investigated Webale's claim, and engage in a short interview to gather facts that are necessary to legal analysis and specific pleading decisions.

WEBCOURSE FOR EXERCISE 2: Please check the **LexisNexis Webcourse** for additional material that may be posted for this exercise.

EXERCISE 2:   JOHN WEBALE v. UNIVERSITY OF WEST DAKOTA [PLEADING PLANNING]

Lawyer's Information

At my supervising associate's instructions, I wrote the following summary of notes I took at an initial interview conducted with Mr. John Webale [hereafter Webale]. This interview occurred at the local clinic where my firm participates as part of its pro bono commitment.

"Mr. Webale is a middle-aged, African-American man who is married and has two children. His wife does not work outside the home. Webale immigrated to this country from Somalia during the strife in that war-torn country in the early 1990s. He settled in West Dakota with a refugee community and last year became a United States citizen. His wife was born and raised in West Dakota, and his children were born here.

Twelve years ago Webale started working at the University of West Dakota [UWD] as a delivery person in the University Stores. In this position, Webale drove trucks ferrying things around campus, and joined the Teamster's Union. He worked the first or early morning shift which was very convenient in terms of participating in parenting his then young children. His work was evaluated as acceptable and he experienced no accidents or disciplinary reports.

One year later, UWD transferred Webale to a job as a custodian with the Parking and Transportation Department. The stated reason for this transfer was listed as "greater need and budgetary cutbacks." Six years after that, UWD told Webale that he would be laid off because his position as a custodian was being abolished due to budget cutbacks. UWD then rescinded the layoff notice because Webale, as a member of the Teamster's Union, was covered by its collective bargaining agreement, and this agreement required that a worker with less security be laid off first. So UWD reassigned Webale to its Fifth Street parking ramp under the Department of Parking and Transportation Services [DPTS].

After this transfer, UWD placed Webale on a third shift [10 p.m. to 6 a.m.] work schedule because of his lack of "clock-time" seniority in this position. Under UWD's administrative rules regarding "clock-time" seniority, Webale's previous seniority at other parts of the University did not count. The Teamster's Union filed an administrative grievance on Webale's behalf arguing that UWD violated Webale's "primary seniority" rights by assigning him to the third shift. Despite the hardships this posed to Webale's family, UWD's Human Resources Review Panel ruled that the collective bargaining agreement did not require management to use prior seniority for shift-changes. It also found that the use of site specific "clock-time" seniority was reasonable. The Teamsters Union did not appeal this determination. Webale did not know the reason why the Union chose not to appeal.

Webale has continued to work as a third shift custodian in the DPTS assigned to the Fifth Street parking ramp. His work performance has been good and he has had no disciplinary problems or other personnel issues. As years went by, Webale sought but did not receive two promotions at UWD. He contends that both denials were based on his race. Two years ago he first applied for an opening as a third-shift general maintenance supervisor at DPTS. UWD's selection process for this position included a panel consisting of the UWD's general maintenance supervisor, the parking area supervisor, and the maintenance supervisor.

Webale indicated that it seemed very difficult for African-Americans to get promoted from custodial to low and mid-level management at UWD. He said that most of his custodian colleagues at DPTS are Black and that many had experienced similar situations. Webale said that he asked the maintenance supervisor why he did not get the first promotion and was told. "The other applicant was more qualified. You people always want to believe there was race involved. There was no race involved in this decision." Webale indicated that he never mentioned race in this brief conversation.

When asked about concrete demonstrations of racially motivated work interactions, Webale shared that while working at the University Stores, Webale's direct supervisor called him "tan" in front of the maintenance manager. This was not the same person who sat on the hiring committee for the first promotion Webale sought. Webale also believes that his supervisor at the Fifth Street Ramp's frequent references to him as a "particular person" are negative, racial remarks, but he has never sought to clarify precisely what his supervisor means by this phrase. Webale has heard two parking attendants at the ramp consistently talking about "all the damn Somalians." He also indicated that former parking lot attendant frequently made derogatory comments about "Black Africans" and occasionally used the "N" word. Webale indicated that none of these remarks were directed to him, and acknowledged that he does not face what he considers a hostile work environment.

After losing out on his second promotion attempt last year, and with the help of the Local Union's Advocacy Unit, Webale filed a discrimination charge with the West Dakota Department of Human Rights [WDDHR] and with the Equal Employment Opportunity Commission [EEOC]. Webale, with help of Teamster's non-legally trained officers, alleged that UWD's failure to promote him and other actions [concerning transfers and seniority denial] were on account of race. Webale claims that a non-lawyer staff member of WDDHR did a perfunctory investigation of this claim. WDDHR issued a written finding that there was no probable cause to believe that UWD had discriminated against Webale and dismissed Webale's claim. The EEOC adopted the findings of the WDDHR and closed Webale's file."

Your supervising associate has asked you to meet with the non-lawyer Union Advocate who helped Webale with his EEOC claim to learn whatever relevant additional information exists. Your supervisor wants your specific recommendations, based on your interview, regarding how the firm should allege the racially discriminatory treatment of Webale in regards to employment promotion. Your supervisor anticipates filing this complaint in the United States District Court for the District of West Dakota. This exercise concerns only asserting a claim under Title VII of the Civil Rights Act of 1964 so do not consider possible claims for deprivation of civil rights under 42 U.S.C. § 1983, or possibilities under West Dakota state law. Assume that discrimination in employment promotion is a valid, well-recognized claim under Title VII precedents. Assume also that West Dakota is located in the new 13th Circuit in the federal court system and has no relevant precedent.

Your assignment is to briefly interview the advocate to develop recommendations regarding how to allege racial discrimination in promotion.

EXERCISE 3: SOME DON'T LIKE IT HOT

FOCUS OF THIS EXERCISE: Drafting a complaint, particularly if pleading is covered before personal and subject matter jurisdiction.

SKILLS INVOLVED: Converting claims to elements, applying federal pleading rules to facts, making strategically sound decisions, and drafting clear, accurate language.

ESTIMATED TIME FOR COMPLETING THIS EXERCISE:

60 to 90 minutes

ESTIMATED LEVEL OF DIFFICULTY: Moderate

YOUR ROLE IN THIS EXERCISE: You will play the role of a lawyer representing Lula Mae Strawder, and draft a short complaint based on the following information: an interviewing memorandum and legal research summary.

WEBCOURSE FOR EXERCISE 3: Please check the **LexisNexis Webcourse** for additional material that may be posted for this exercise.

EXERCISE 3:   SOME DON'T LIKE IT HOT

Assume that having recently graduated and passed the Columbia bar exam, you have a solo practice in University City. Lula Mae Strawder recently hired you to represent her interests concerning the following matter. This is how you summarized your initial interview in a file memorandum:

Ms. Lula Mae Strawder met with me today. She was very upset with recent interactions with Dutchess Power and Light [DPL], the large, bureaucratic private utilities company that apparently cares little about alienating its customers in University City. Ms. Strawder indicated that she had utilities with DPL eight years ago when she resided in Campus Flats, a large apartment complex near the University. She said she cancelled her services by a telephone call, effective the day she moved to St. Petersburg, Florida, to accept a new job. The representative from DPL with whom she spoke that day assured her that the call was sufficient to stop utility services, and that the representative would enter a termination order regarding this cancellation after the call that would become effective on the designated date.

Ms. Strawder returned to University City last month as apparently neither the Florida job nor the relationship that lured her away worked out. She returned to Campus Flats and opened a new account with DPL in her name, the same name she used previously. She paid the required deposit to protect against unpaid bills, and an estimated first month's service charge. Two weeks later, without notice, her utilities service was stopped. This shut-off occurred at noon on a day during the hottest period on record. Columbia, like much of the rest of the world, struggles with increasingly warm temperatures while politicians dither about whether climate change exists.

Ms. Strawder's youngest son, Timothy, suffers from an asthmatic condition requiring daily use of an electronic inhalator, and she had to take him to the emergency room that evening. Timothy was ultimately hospitalized for a day. Ms. Strawder moved Timothy to her sister's apartment in University City when he was released from the hospital. Timothy stayed there until she was able to persuade DPL to restore utilities service one week later. Ms, Strawder also has been assured that Timothy suffered no permanent harm from this event, and he is doing well now. Ms. Strawder's emergency room and hospital expenses were $4856. Lula Mae is one of the many million Americans with no health insurance.

Ms. Strawder also lost everything in her refrigerator as all of the food spoiled during the one week of intense heat without electricity. Considering staples plus perishables, she estimates losing approximately $380 worth of food.

Ms. Strawder learned after her utilities were shut-off that an unpaid balance had accumulated on her first account. Apparently, DPL had neglected to discontinue services to her former apartment, and a new tenant ran up three months of charges before skipping out on his lease. Ms. Strawder did not know the name of this person, and has made no attempt to ascertain his or her identity or whereabouts. With interest and penalties, the amount owing on that debt is now allegedly $6,212.17. Ms. Strawder indicated that she had paid her account in full by writing a check and mailing it the day she moved out. She does not keep check records.

Ms. Strawder said that she started asking, and then begging, DPL to restore her power as soon as she realized that it was not the result of a falling tree. She fully advised DPL representatives within 4 hours of the cutoff. The DPL representatives with whom she communicated after her power was stopped were insensitive, stubborn, and rude. She indicated that she was only able to restore current service by signing an agreement to repay the alleged debt on the account. She said she would not have done so except her sister was going out of town and she needed to bring Timothy back home. She said she wrote the words "under protest" on the document that she signed. She did not, however, keep the copy of this document even though DPL gave her one.

Ms. Strawder is one of the "other Americans" about whom politicians occasionally prattle. No rising economic tide has lifted her boat. She struggles to survive and support Timothy and his older daughter, Tabitha, on a job that pays slightly above minimum wage.

Assume that after this interview, you called DPL several times. They never let you go above "regional assistant manager" level, whatever that is. You never got to speak to a lawyer, and you don't know whether they have in-house counsel. These calls primarily confirmed Ms. Strawder's negative characterizations of DPL's customer service personnel. You learned that DPL has done nothing to try to collect this obligation from the tenant who received services after moving into Ms. Strawder's vacated apartment. You got the sense that DPL did not even know about this successor tenant until you told them, and that they had no plans to or policies requiring pursuing this option. You also learned that DPL denies any liability or responsibility for damages caused by their terminating power, contending that their application contract contains a clause authorizing shut-off without notice if an unpaid balance exceeding $1,000 exists.

DPL practically invited you to sue them. After counseling Ms. Strawder fully about the advantages and disadvantages of suing, she decided to accept DPL's invitation.

Your research indicates the following: [and please assume that this is all the law that potentially applies to Ms. Strawder's situation; do not spend any time doing any additional research].

Perhaps not surprising considering the political clout of energy related industries in today's world, no Columbia statutes, rules, or administrative regulations apply to this situation. What does seem surprising is that DPL has no internal regulations regarding utility terminations. Deregulation stemming from an all government is bad mentality apparently governs Columbia's utilities industry.

Columbia's statute of limitations for debt collection is its general contract provision of six years. Cases indicate that this statute starts running when the debt arises, i.e. when the due date of a required payment on a service contract passes without debtor compliance.

Columbia also has an unfair consumer collection practices act, Colum. Stat. 559.55 through 559.785. This act prohibits conduct when collecting alleged debts that can reasonably be expected to harass debtors and their families. This statute defines "debt or consumer debt" to mean "any obligation or alleged obligation of a consumer to pay money arising out of a transaction in which the money, property, insurance, or services which are the subject of the transaction are primarily for personal, family, or household purposes, whether or not such obligation has been reduced to judgment," 559.55(1).

Section 559.72 lists generally prohibited practices. The one that arguably applies to Ms. Strawder's situation is subsection (9) which says "no person shall . . . claim, attempt, or threaten to enforce a debt when such person knows that the debt is not legitimate or assert the existence of some other legal right when such person knows that the right does not exist."

Section 559.77(2), concerning legal remedies, provides "upon adverse adjudication, the defendant shall be liable for actual damages and for additional statutory damages of up to $1,000, together with court costs and reasonable attorney's fees incurred by the plaintiff." The attorney's fee-shifting provision is very important because Ms. Strawder does not have the financial ability to pay you a reasonable hourly fee for the amount of time this lawsuit might require.

The Columbia Rules of Civil Procedure follow the Federal Rules of Civil Procedure verbatim. Assume that the appropriate state court is the District Court for Maplewood County, Columbia, and the appropriate federal court is the United States District Court for the Middle District of Columbia. Your assignment is to draft a complaint that asserts Ms. Strawder's legal claims in this situation. Please ensure that your draft runs no more than three pages.

EXERCISE 4: SAM ADAMS

FOCUS OF THIS EXERCISE: Draft a complaint, particularly if pleading is covered after personal and subject matter jurisdiction.

SKILLS INVOLVED: Converting claims to elements, applying federal complaint pleading rules to facts, making appropriate strategic decisions, and drafting clear, accurate complaint language.

ESTIMATED TIME FOR COMPLETING THIS EXERCISE:

60 to 90 minutes

ESTIMATED LEVEL OF DIFFICULTY: Moderate

YOUR ROLE IN THIS EXERCISE: You will play the role of a lawyer representing Sam Adams, and draft a short complaint based on the information you learned interviewing him and the following legal research summary.

WEBCOURSE FOR EXERCISE 4: Please check the **LexisNexis Webcourse** for additional material that may be posted for this exercise.

EXERCISE 4:   SAM ADAMS

Pleading Drafting

Assume that you are a lawyer who has just begun practicing in University City, Columbia. One of your first clients is Sam Adams. Adams was very angry about his situation during your interview. Adams owns a 1994 Classic Porsche car that burst into fire and burned severely two weeks ago. This fire happened just one week after had taken his car in for repairs by the Bill Blair Auto Classic Repair Shop just across the state line in River City, Georgia. Adams now wants to pursue all legal remedies that he has against Blair.

The problem with the car began when Adams noticed a small puddle of gas on his driveway underneath the car. Adams assumed that the car had a gas leak so he took the car into Bill Blair's shop that same morning. Blair checked him in personally and Adams described the problem and asked Blair to do whatever was necessary to repair it. Adams also signed the standard service order form that most car repair shops in University City use. Adams then walked to work.

Adams picked up his car that same day and paid Blair $551.65 for his services. The service order indicates that a leak in the fuel line was repaired and that approximately seven feet were replaced and clamped. The order specified two hours of labor at $200.00, parts (fuel line and clamps) in the amount of $351.65, and tax. Adams paid this bill by check and drove off.

Unlike many classic car owners, Adams drives his car as regular transportation and does not treat the vehicle as a collectible asset kept mostly in a garage. Adams used the car normally for the next week which meant that he only drove it to and from work and around University City. Adams estimates that he put approximately 100 to 150 miles on the car during the week. Adams neither smelled gas nor noticed any further evidence of a gas leak during this time. Adams did not inspect the work done by Blair or Blair's employees. Adams lacks mechanical knowledge and skills and so did not crawl under the car to view the gas line after its repair because he would not have known what he was seeing.

Adams had an unexpected holiday on the day of the accident and he persuaded a friend to take the day off from work so that they could go to the beach. They packed the Porsche with camping equipment. They then drove east on N.W. 8th Avenue on their way out of town. As Adams was accelerating up the steep hill on N.W. 8th Avenue between N.W. 23rd Street and N.W. 22nd Street, his car lost power and then shut down. Adams first smelled smoke and then he saw it pouring through the car vents "from everywhere." Adams then looked in his rear view mirror and saw black smoke billowing from the rear of car. Just before the peak of the hill, Adams pulled over to the right side of the highway, jumped the curb, and pulled on the emergency brake. Adam's friend opened the car door, looked out to the rear, and screamed, "The car is on fire!" Adams and his friend got out of the car safely. No one was injured. Adams then looked under the car and saw a pool of flames. Adams also saw dripping, burning gas and a fuel line hanging to the ground.

A pedestrian ran into a nearby house and called the Fire Department. The Fire Department arrived in three minutes while traffic eastbound on N.W. 8th Avenue was blocked by the Police Department. The Fire Department put out the fire and then Adams had the car towed back to his apartment.

You inspected the car and confirmed that it is worth nothing but salvage value. The engine is a charred, unusable mass of metal. The underneath of the car is burned so badly that it is impossible to determine where the fire started. Everyone you have consulted, however, believes that this fire was caused by a gas line leak which somehow ignited. Apparently, this automobile model has 15 feet of fuel line. Most of it is under the car but a very small portion of it is in the engine. Adams' car has a blue book value of $112,000 and you have had a reliable salvage estimate on it of about $200.

It cost Adams $155 to tow the car back to his home. Adams also had to live for nine days without an automobile until Adams bought a replacement. Adams had to take busses to work during this interim period. Adams' estimates spending approximately $50 on bus fares during the nine days that he was without a car.

Your investigation indicates that this model Porsches catch fire with some frequency. A mechanic at another shop specializing in classic vehicles told you that it was his practice to replace all fuel lines on these vehicles when they got old to prevent just such a fire. Adams bought this car new in 1994 and he has owned it since then. The car has about 76,000 miles on it. Adams checked his repair records and found that he has never had any work done on the fuel lines before this.

Adams received no warning, either written or oral, from Blair or any of Blair's employees regarding the necessity of replacing more fuel lines. Adams says that he would have done whatever was necessary to make his classic car run again in a safe manner. Adams also did not place any cost limit on the amount of work Blair could perform.

You called Blair to discuss the incident and he was not responsive. He indicated that he did not have insurance at the time of this repair because of a clerical screw up so this case is not just a simple matter of shifting liability to a deeper pocket. Blair got very defensive when you suggested the possibility of litigation unless Adams was promptly "made whole." He said there was "no way in hell that he was going to settle" because he didn't do anything wrong. He also said that Adams "doesn't have a case."

Investigation indicates that Blair's shop is a corporation. It is incorporated in Georgia and has its principal place of business in River City. The business name is Bill Blair Auto Repair, Ltd.

Your legal research produced the following file memorandum:

"The most promising remedy is negligence. This requires showing that Bill Blair Auto Repair had a duty to protect Adams from the injury; that it failed to perform that duty; and that the damage that Adams suffered resulted from that failure. Negligently repairing a motor vehicle has been recognized as a valid cause of action in many states including Columbia. *Bill Kelley Chevrolet v. Kerr.*

Our inability to prove specific acts of negligence by Blair in repairing our client's gas lines may not be fatal because we can argue that the doctrine of *res ipsa loquitor* applies. In *Stanek v. Houston*, a truck mysteriously went out of control, careened about 300 feet off the highway, and finally stopped inside a restaurant where it injured the plaintiff who was chopping onions. The Court there permitted the use of the doctrine of *res ipsa loquitor* stating:

> "This doctrine is a rule of evidence, applicable when the following conditions are met: (1) the instrumentality involved was within the exclusive control of the defendant at the time of the injury, both as to operation and inspection; (2) the injury was not the result of any voluntary action or contribution on the part of the Plaintiff; and (3) the action would not have occurred had the Defendant used due care. *Res ipsa* is sometimes said to raise a refutable presumption of negligence, but under the law this state and some other jurisdictions, it merely establishes a permissible inference which may be rejected by the jury."

In *Yarbrough v. Ball U-Drive Systems, Inc.*, the Columbia Supreme Court held that *res ipsa's* requirement of exclusive control by the defendant does not mean that the defendant has to be in control of the motor vehicle at the time of the injury. There the Plaintiff rented a truck from Defendant and drove it 100 miles, unloaded it, and started back. He had traveled about 20 miles back when the truck's rear end flew into the air and then turned over two or three times. Plaintiff was pinned underneath the truck and killed. The Court held that the fact that the Defendant had control of the truck up to the very time it was entrusted to Yarbrough was sufficient to satisfy this requirement of *res ipsa loquitor.*

The Columbia Court of Appeal reached the same decision in a negligent repair case in *Bill Kelley Chevrolet, Inc. v. Kerr, supra.* There *res ipsa loquitor* was applied to an accident caused when a truck accelerated unexpectedly after its accelerator spring broke. The evidence showed that the accelerator spring broke at a point where it had been crimped or bent out of its normal shape. This accident occurred after the vehicle had been driven only 15 to 20 miles after the motor had been worked on at the Defendant's garage. During the course of the Defendant's repairs, a mechanic employed by the Defendant had removed or disconnected the spring and reconnected it.

Three fire cases from other jurisdictions may also be helpful. In The *Automobile Insurance Company of Hartford v. Williams*, a District of Columbia decision, the plaintiff brought his new Buick, which was less than a few months old, in for a major motor tune-up because he was preparing for a trip to Florida. After driving away from the defendant's shop he noticed a very strong odor of gasoline. The next morning, he started the motor and left the car running to let it warm up. A moment later flames appeared beneath the hood and by the time firemen arrived the motor had been completely destroyed. The Court held that the Plaintiff was entitled to get to the jury on these facts, stating:

> "Courts will take judicial notice that gasoline vapors are highly inflammable and even explosive, and that this characteristic combined with the spark from

the electrical system provides the force which propels an automobile. The courts will also take judicial notice that automobile motors in a proper state of repair do not burst into flames."

In Sam *White Oldsmobile Co. v. Jones Apothecary, Inc.*, a Texas decision, the Plaintiff proved that in the three weeks before the accident the Defendant had made a number of repairs on the automobile which included several items which required work in the wiring system under the dashboard. The fire started under the dashboard. Affirming a judgment for the Plaintiff, the Court held that while no one testified positively how the fire started, the evidence showed that in all probability it did result from a defective wiring system and that this defective condition was due to the failure of the Defendant to make the necessary repairs.

Finally, in *Wartell v. Hartford Insurance Co.*, a Louisiana Court found liability when an improper oil filter was installed and the Plaintiff's car subsequently caught fire and burned.

Another possibility here is Blair's failure to warn Adams either that his car was not fully repaired or that there were other possible causes of gas leaks that might make his car unsafe to drive. Research disclosed no cases of negligent repair that discuss such a failure to warn. Nevertheless, it arguably constitutes actionable negligence. For example, in *Orkin Exterminating Co., Inc. v. Culpepper*, the trial court found liability for negligent failure to warn. Here an exterminating company knew of earlier burglaries of homes which were covered by the tent used by that company and failed to warn the Plaintiff of the previous break-ins. The Court of Appeal upheld the trial court's decision that a valid cause of action was stated and proved for negligently failing to warn the Plaintiff of the danger.

Including specific acts of negligence in our complaint does not prevent us from taking advantage of *res ipsa loquitor.* In *Cortez Roofing Inc. v. Barolo*, the Supreme Court stated:

"The fact that specific allegations of negligence are also made could not, in itself, preclude the application of *res ipsa loquitor* since Columbia follows the rule that, in a proper case, proof of specific acts of negligence does not forestall a Plaintiff from relying on the doctrine."

Your assignment is to draft a complaint for Adams. The rules of civil procedure for the State of Columbia are identical to the federal rules of civil procedure. In addition, University City is in the Southern District of the State of Columbia and River City is in the Northern District of Georgia.

Chapter 8

DISCOVERY

INTRODUCTION

Lawyers engage in extensive planning and strategic thinking implementing and responding to pre-trial civil discovery initiatives. These procedures permit or require exchange of information, documents, and tangible things after pleading and before trying claims and defenses. Spanning thirteen Federal Rules, countless local court procedures, and numerous related state evidential and privilege statutes, discovery supplies the most important phase of civil litigation. Outcomes during discovery profoundly influence consensual dispute resolution via negotiation and mediation, and pre-trial disposition via summary judgment. Probably the greatest single innovation in the Federal Rules, discovery procedures allow learning virtually all non-privileged information relevant to claims and defenses that is proportional to the needs and contexts lawsuits present.

Navigating discovery practice skillfully requires mastering and applying a plethora of technical general federal and local court rules concerning the six primary tools for getting and giving information. These information transmission tools include live oral testimony through depositions; written responses to written inquiries through interrogatories, depositions by written questions: written requests to admit; production of documents, electronically stored information, and tangible things; land entry for inspection and other purposes; and physical and mental examinations. Using and responding to the various ways these tools can be integrated and implemented demands careful planning and skillful negotiating because all these tools are designed to be self-executing. The system's reliance on extra-judicial implementation creates multiple opportunities to cooperate, collaborate, and compete in pre-trial interactions.

Contemporary discovery knowledge applications also require attending to mandatory information disclosure and production at three pre-trial stages: initially after pleadings generally end; information regarding expert witnesses at least 90 days before trial; and specifically ordered pre-trial information transfers shortly before trial. Planning and implementing these exchanges typically includes multiple negotiations with lawyers representing other litigation participants and judges or magistrates before and during many discovery and scheduling conferences that the expanding emphasis on judicial case management, discussed elsewhere, frequently generates.

Applied planning requires attending to all elements of legal claims and defenses raised in pleadings and how they can be proved or rebutted, and to collateral information that can be used to enhance [via bolstering credibility] or discredit [via impeachment] persuasive stories. Following this blueprint tracks the fundamental requirement that discoverable evidence must be relevant to claims and defenses. Only information and evidence tending to make claims more or less likely, and information regarding credibility factors, is discoverable. Recognized evidential privileges supply another discovery limit and prevent disclosure of relevant information and evidence that qualifies for attorney-client, doctor-patient, and other contexts where policy decisions to protect this information control. Effective, accurate decisions also must be made regarding a specific litigation-linked doctrine that provides qualified immunity from discovery for documents and tangible things prepared in anticipation of litigation. Generally, this type of information and evidence, labeled work product, can be discovered only by showing a substantial need for it, and an inability to acquire this data by other means without substantial hardship. Mental impressions, opinions, and conclusions of attorneys, however, are usually immunized notwithstanding work product *provisions*.

Rapid growth of electronically stored information in numerous formats has generated many novel and challenging contexts for applying discovery knowledge and skill. These applications require finding out what types of electronically stored information clients and adversaries have, where it is kept, how it is kept, and how easy it can be accessed, searched and shared. It requires understanding clients' data retention architecture and communicating clearly with technical people to ensure that relevant information is not destroyed creating spoliation issues that often overwhelm merits of claims and defenses. It creates numerous opportunities to dispute and occasionally creatively resolve expense and cost-sharing issues concerning information that is not easily accessible. It also creates opportunities to invoke a relatively recent new discovery limit that allows courts to protect otherwise relevant, non-privileged information that they deem presents more burden or expense to exchange than is warranted by its likely benefit.

Finally, lawyers must apply their discovery knowledge, strategy, and skill in adversarial contexts which many contend create economic incentives that make extensive abuse of non-refereed processes inevitable. Choices in these contexts often trigger challenging ethical dilemmas and applications of discovery sanctioning rules.

EXERCISE 1: JOHN WEBALE v. UNIVERSITY OF WEST DAKOTA [DISCOVERY RESPONSE INVESTIGATION]

FOCUS OF THIS EXERCISE: Interview client's employee who prepared a potentially important document.

SKILLS INVOLVED: Interviewing to gather facts regarding how to respond to anticipated discovery initiatives regarding a potentially damaging email document and understanding relationships between fact collection, discovery and ethical rules.

ESTIMATED TIME FOR COMPLETING THIS EXERCISE:

60 minutes

ESTIMATED LEVEL OF DIFFICULTY: Somewhat difficult

YOUR ROLE IN THIS EXERCISE: Play the role of either a lawyer representing the University of West Dakota defending an employment discrimination claim, or a University employee who recently wrote a grant compliance report that may contain damaging data, at a brief interview.

WEBCOURSE FOR EXERCISE 1: Please check the **LexisNexis Webcourse** for additional material that may be posted for this exercise.

EXERCISE 1: JOHN WEBALE v. UNIVERSITY OF WEST DAKOTA

Discovery Investigation

You are the lawyer defending UWD against Webale's claim in federal court for racial employment promotion discrimination. Yesterday, your supervising attorney sent you the following email regarding this case:

Internal University of West Dakota network email

To: You
From: Supervising attorney

Re: E-mail document investigation

I need you to look into an email document prepared by Andy Andrews, a non-lawyer who works in the University's Department of Sponsored Research, regarding Webale's claim of racially discriminatory failure to promote. I don't have a lot of the specifics so I think a face-to-face meeting with Andrews is necessary. What I know is that the Northern Rockies Educational Consortium administers US Department of Education grants, and the University of West Dakota has several such awards. Apparently at least one of them requires reporting employment statistics every two years. According to Andrews, a recently prepared report shows bad numbers for us regarding Webale's claim. After reading about Webale's suit in the local newspaper, Andrews sent our office an email asking what s/he should do with this report. Although this email purported to attach the report, it was not attached. Neither I nor anyone in the University Counsel's office has seen this report, and none of us know anything more about this situation.

So I need you to discuss this report thoroughly with Andrews. After that discussion, I need to know the following: (1) whether we need to unilaterally disclose this report; and (2) if not, what, if anything, can we do successfully to block producing this report in the event Webale's lawyer seeks production with a description sufficiently encompassing it. I am also wondering whether Andrews' act of sending it on to us gives us a privilege claim.

Thanks. You are doing good work, and it's great to have you in our office.

Your assignment is to conduct a conversation with Andy [short for either Andrew or Andrea] Andrews investigating the topics your supervising attorney identified and anything else that seems pertinent.

EXERCISE 2: ABLE v. BUCKWOOD MEADOWS
[TAKING A DEPOSITION]

FOCUS OF THIS EXERCISE: Depose the plaintiff only on liability issues.

SKILLS INVOLVED: Applying law and deposition rules to facts, asking questions, listening, and organizing inquiry appropriately.

ESTIMATED TIME FOR COMPLETING THIS EXERCISE:

60 minutes

ESTIMATED LEVEL OF DIFFICULTY: Somewhat easy

YOUR ROLE IN THIS EXERCISE: You will play either the role of a lawyer representing the defendant, *Able v. Buckwoods Meadows* in this negligence claim, or the Plaintiff, Alex Able, and engage in a short portion of a deposition focused solely on liability issues concerning Alex's slip and fall in Defendant's restaurant.

WEB COURSE FOR EXERCISE 2: Please check the web course for additional material that may be posted for this exercise.

EXERCISE 2: ABLE v. BUCKWOOD MEADOWS [TAKING A DEPOSITION]

Case Pleading File

IN THE EIGHTH JUDICIAL CIRCUIT COURT OF WEST DAKOTA

ALEX ABLE,

Plaintiff,

vs.

Case No. 123456

BUCKWOOD MEADOWS, INC.
d/b/a Dew Drop Inn of
University City,
Defendant.

COMPLAINT FOR DAMAGES

Plaintiff, ALEX ABLE, sues Defendant, BUCKWOOD MEADOWS, INC, and alleges:

1. This is an action for damages that exceeds $15,000.
2. On the 16th day of May, one year ago, Plaintiff was a guest at the DEW DROP INN, of University City, a restaurant owned and operated by Defendant.
3. On that date, the Defendant had carpet in the hallway from its dining area to public rest rooms.
4. While walking on this carpet in this hallway in from the dining room of the Defendant's restaurant, Plaintiff tripped and fell on this carpet and fell to the floor.
5. Plaintiff's fall was a direct and proximate result of the negligence of Defendant in negligently installing and maintaining this carpet in its publicly accessible premises, and allowing a hazardous condition in this carpet to exist without taking remedies to correct same; and failing to warn guests of the hidden hazardous condition in its carpet.
6. As a direct and proximate result of the negligence of the Defendant, Plaintiff sustained a compression fracture of her back; and her injuries are permanent and partially disabling.
7. Plaintiff has been required to submit to numerous and extensive x-rays, examinations and therapy treatments including the taking of drugs in an effort to combat the pain from which she has suffered; she has suffered a loss of earnings to date hereof in the approximate sum of twenty thousand dollars ($20,000) and she also has sustained a permanent impairment of her earnings capacity; and she continues to suffer from pain, shock, nervous reaction and inconvenience for which she should be compensated.

WHEREFORE, Plaintiff demands judgment against the Defendant for the foregoing damages, a jury trial, the costs of this action, and whatever additional relief this Court may deem appropriate.

Respectfully submitted,
STRIKE, EARLY & OFTEN, P.A.

IN THE EIGHTH JUDICIAL CIRCUIT COURT OF WEST DAKOTA

ALEX ABLE,

Plaintiff,

vs.

BUCKWOOD MEADOWS, INC.
d/b/a Dew Drop Inn of
University City,
Defendant.

Case No. 123456
Division: C

DEFENDANT'S MOTION TO DISMISS

Defendant, BUCKWOOD MEADOWS, INC., respectfully requests this Court to dismiss the Plaintiff's Complaint for Damages filed against it, and, as grounds, states:

1. The Plaintiff's Complaint for Damages contains only conclusory allegations that fail to support plausible inferences that it has a claim on which it is entitled to relief.

WHEREFORE, Defendant respectfully moves that the complaint be dismissed.

Respectfully submitted,
Don Kingsfield Attorney for
Defendant 402 Madison Avenue
University City, West Dakota
[assume appropriate zip code
and phone number]

CERTIFICATE OF SERVICE

I HEREBY CERTIFY that a copy of the foregoing Answer has been served [etc]

IN THE EIGHTH JUDICIAL CIRCUIT COURT OF WEST DAKOTA

ALEX ABLE,

Plaintiff,

vs.   Case No. 123456

BUCKWOOD MEADOWS, INC.   Division: C
d/b/a Dew Drop Inn of
University City,
Defendant.

ORDER DENYING DEFENDANT'S MOTION TO DISMISS

This cause was heard on the Defendant's Motion to Dismiss the Plaintiff's Complaint. This Court, after hearing argument of counsel and being otherwise fully advised, hereby ORDERS:

1. The Defendant's Motion to Dismiss is denied.

2. The Defendant is given 15 days from the date of this order to answer the Plaintiff's complaint.

DONE AND ORDERED in Chambers in University City, West Dakota, this [assume appropriate date]

Circuit Judge

Copies furnished to:

John Strike, Attorney for Plaintiff

Don Kingsfield, Attorney for Defendant

IN THE EIGHTH JUDICIAL CIRCUIT COURT OF WEST DAKOTA

ALEX ABLE,

Plaintiff,

vs.

BUCKWOOD MEADOWS, INC.
d/b/a Dew Drop Inn of
University City,
Defendant.

Case No. 123456
Division: C

DEFENDANT'S ANSWER TO PLAINTIFF'S COMPLAINT FOR DAMAGES

Defendant, BUCKWOOD MEADOWS, INC., d/b/a Dew Drop Inn of University City, answers Plaintiff's Complaint for Damages as follows:

1. Answering paragraphs two, three four, and five of the complaint, Defendant admits that on May 16, one year ago, Plaintiff fell at the Dew Drop Inn, however Defendant denies remaining allegations contained in these paragraphs.

2. Answering paragraphs six and seven of the complaint, Defendant is without knowledge as to the truth of the allegations contained therein and, therefore, denies them.

AFFIRMATIVE DEFENSE

3. Defendant further avers and says that the incident and any resulting damage or injury as a consequence thereof was caused by the negligence of the Plaintiff, which proximately contributed thereto, and which either bars or proportionately reduces any recovery of damages from Defendant.

WHEREFORE, Defendant having fully answered Plaintiff's Complaint prays that it be dismissed and that Defendant go hence without cost.

> Respectfully submitted,
> Don Kingsfield, Attorney for
> Defendant,
> 402 Madison Avenue University City,
> West Dakota [assume appropriate zip
> code and phone number]

CERTIFICATE OF SERVICE

I HEREBY CERTIFY that a copy of the foregoing Answer has been served upon [etc.]

EXERCISE 3: SANDY SPRINGS v. RUST-NOT ALUMINUM CO.

FOCUS OF THIS EXERCISE: Draft three requests to admit on behalf of assigned client; three responses to requests drafted by students who represent the other litigant; draft and argue all necessary discovery enforcement motions; and negotiate case once this written discovery is concluded.

SKILLS INVOLVED: Applying rules 36 and 37 to a factual scenario, drafting effective requests to admit and responses, exercising strategic skills linking discovery tools to negotiation objectives, and preparing and presenting short negotiation of a simple case.

ESTIMATED TIME FOR COMPLETING THIS EXERCISE: Three hours [60 minutes preparing, 60 minutes drafting and responding to requests to admit, and 60 minutes negotiating]

ESTIMATED LEVEL OF DIFFICULTY: Somewhat difficult

YOUR ROLE IN THIS EXERCISE: You will play the role of a lawyer representing either Sandy Springs or Rust-Not Aluminum Company, in this dog bite claim, and following distributed confidential information, draft three requests to admit, respond to three requests submitted by the lawyer representing the other client in your pair, draft and handle all enforcement motions that may result, and then negotiate for no more than an hour seeking an agreement resolving all claims.

WEBCOURSE FOR EXERCISE 3: Please check the **LexisNexis Webcourse** for additional material that may be posted for this exercise.

EXERCISE 3:   SPRINGS v. RUST-NOT ALUMINUM COMPANY

Sandy Springs has filed a lawsuit in the Circuit Court for the Eighth Judicial Circuit of Columbia, in and for Alachua County, Columbia, against the Rust-Not Aluminum Company. His complaint alleges dog bite liability under Columbia Statutes and it seeks damages "in excess of $15,000" for medical expenses, lost wages, and pain and suffering. It also seeks a jury trial.

This suit was filed over a year ago and three depositions have been taken. The important information from them follows in narrative form.

You will be paired with another student and asked to represent either the plaintiff of the defendant in this case. Your first task is to prepare three requests for admission. You must give these questions to the student representing your adversary. Then you will need to respond to the request served on you and provide your opponent with a copy of your questions.

You must not discuss or share this information with anyone. Please do not spend more than one hour each preparing and drafting your admissions, drafting your responses, and negotiating.

After the admissions have been drafted, served, and answered, you will be asked to assume that a pre-trial conference has been set in this case. Judge Unfriendly, the Circuit Judge assigned to this suit, has let it be known that he strongly desires to conclude all of his pending jury trials within the next three months. He then will rotate into a criminal law docket, and he does not intend to transfer any civil jury trials to colleagues. A copy of his Order Setting the Pre-Trial Conference follows, and pay particular attention to paragraph 5 mandating negotiation.

No formal settlement discussions have been initiated yet in this matter. Both sides, however, have agreed to confer to comply with paragraph 5 and to discuss whether a compromise is possible in this lawsuit before further expenses are incurred. Your next task will be to conduct that negotiation conference.

Your negotiation must be limited to no more than one hour. If you reach a settlement, please prepare a short document reflecting your agreement. This paper does not need to be in any formal form but it must be signed by both lawyers. This document must also be submitted before the announced deadline. If you and your adversary cannot reach a settlement of this dispute within one hour, terminate your negotiation. You then must draft and submit your pre-trial compliance document following Judge Unfriendly's Pre-Trial Conference Order.

Everyone in this class will be negotiating the same problem which mandates that you work alone on this exercise. Do not discuss it, share your plans or preparations for it, or share your experiences with it with anyone else in the class.

Narrative Summary of Sandy Springs Deposition

My name is Sandy Springs and I am the plaintiff in this lawsuit. I am 19 years old and I work at the Moulde Print Shop as a typesetter. I was attacked by two Doberman pincher dogs while riding my bicycle in a northerly direction on northeast 19th street just north of N.E. 32nd Avenue in Columbia City. This attack occurred at approximately 7:00 a.m. on [assume appropriate date].

I was on my way to work that morning when I was attacked. I ordinarily do not ride on N.E. 19th Street but I decided to go that way for a change of scenery. I was riding on the right hand side of the road and I was riding slowly because I had a lot of time before I was due at work. My work did not start until 7:30 a.m. and I was only 15 minutes away from my office.

I first noticed the dogs when they were in the driveway in front of the Rust-Not Aluminum Company building. Dogs scare me, particularly big dogs. These dogs were big and they were not leashed. I was even with them when they suddenly ran out after me. They were barking, sounding and looking mean. I did not do anything to provoke them. I did not say anything to attract them to me. They attacked me. Each of them bit me on my legs as they chased me while I was riding my bicycle.

One of them then got tangled up in my front wheel and I had to stop my bicycle. I got off my bike, picked it up and held it in front of me, and then started swinging it in a semi-circular fashion in front of me to keep the dogs from biting me again. The dogs retreated to just out of the range of my swinging bike, and they continued to circle me looking at me angrily. They were barking and baring their teeth. It was a terrifying situation. My legs were in pain and I could feel that I was bleeding.

I noticed a man, who I now know to be Ted Timid, the dogs' owner, walking toward me and the dogs. He was walking slowly as if he had all the time in the world. He yelled at me to put the bicycle down because I might hurt the dogs. I told him I would put the bicycle down only when I was safe. He came up near the dogs and they did not bother him at all. They acted like they knew him.

When he got next to me, he asked me again to put the bicycle down. I told him I would not until I was safe. He said that he would restrain the dogs if I stopped swinging the bike. He also said that swinging the bicycle was making it worse because it was making the dogs angry. I said they were pretty angry before because they bit me and knocked me off my bike.

Since I had no other choice, I lowered the bicycle to the ground. Immediately Timid grabbed the collars of both of the dogs and pulled the dogs back toward the driveway in front of the Rust-Not building. I got on my bicycle and rode quickly away from there. About three seconds later, I heard the dogs barking and turned around and they were chasing me again. Then I heard a loud command, "come," which I assume came from Timid. The dogs stopped chasing me and returned in the direction of the Rust-Not Aluminum Company building. I kept on peddling away as fast as I could.

After I had gone a couple of blocks, I stopped, got off my bike, rolled up my trousers, and looked at my legs. I saw that I was bleeding heavily in both legs. I had two wounds on my right calf and one wound on my left calf. My pants and socks were bloody. I started to feel dizzy.

Not knowing what to do, I continued on to work. My boss saw me and I explained to him what happened. Then I fainted.

My boss took me to the emergency room at County General Hospital. I revived in the car on the way. At the hospital my wounds were cleaned by a nurse and I was told to wait there. A young, nervous looking, doctor came in and asked me what happened. I told him.

After waiting another hour, I was given bandages for the two wounds on my right and left legs. I was given no pain killer. I had no stitches. My leg throbbed with pain off and on throughout this entire experience.

I also received an initial rabies inoculation at the emergency room. It was very painful. I then learned for the first time that there was nothing I could do but wait for a week to see if the dogs were rabid. If they were, I was told I faced a series of painful but very necessary shots. If I did not get those, I was told that I might die. This frightened me and made me anxious. This was the first time I had ever faced the fact of my death. I had trouble sleeping until I learned that the dogs were not rabid.

I did not work the rest of the week because of the pain and shock and anxiety. I took aspirin for the pain. I had no prescription painkillers. It hurt to stand and to walk so I spent the week in bed. I was able to return to work the following week but it was painful. The pain finally subsided about three weeks after the attack.

I refuse, on advice of counsel, to answer my questions about my use of drugs generally and marijuana specifically. I do drink alcohol occasionally. I had not had anything to drink the morning these dogs attacked me.

I lost wages in the amount of $750.00 for my 5 days of missed work. This is a net figure because I take home $150.00 a day from my job. My total medical expenses were $813.00. I did not have any insurance to cover this loss. It is not paid.

The dogs that attacked me were full grown, adult Dobermans. I do not know their sex. They are the kind of dogs that you usually see as security dogs around businesses. The Rust-Not Aluminum Company does not have a security fence. I assume that the Dobermans performed a security function for the business.

Narrative Summary of Ted Timid's Deposition

My name is Ted Timid. I am 55 years of age, and I work for the Rust-Not Aluminum Company. I work for them as a general secretary and clerk. My working hours are the hours that the business is in operation; that is, from eight in the morning until six in the evening. I do not work for Rust-Not as a night watchman. I do not perform any security functions for them.

Buck Braggart, the manager of Rust-Not, is a personal friend. Two years ago I was down on my luck, and he gave me a job and a place to put my trailer. He let me move my trailer on a vacant piece of land just north of the Rust-Not Aluminum Company building. I live in that trailer now, and I have lived there for two years.

Before this, I worked at the Urban Drive-In Theater in Columbia City. I sold tickets and did general maintenance and cleaning up work. I was there every night that the theater was open. I lived in my trailer on a back part of the lot behind the screen.

Two adult Doberman pincher dogs live with me in the trailer. No one else does. I purchased these dogs as puppies, and keep them for companionship and as household pets. One is six year old male and the other is a seven year old female.

These dogs are not security, guard, or watch dogs. They do not work for Rust-Not. They do not patrol the premises after hours. They do not perform any other security function for Rust-Not. They stay with me, and are in the trailer at all times unless I am walking them outside of it.

These dogs have gentle dispositions. Neither of them has received attack training. Both have been to obedience school and have learned to obey heel, come, and stop commands off leash. They have never bitten anyone except me, playfully. Each has bitten me once, playfully, when I played rough with them. My injuries were minor each time.

My typical routine is to walk these dogs early in the morning after I have awaked and had my breakfast. I do this before I go to work, and I lock them inside my trainer while I am at work. I will usually let them out at noon because I eat my lunch at home. I don't have much money. Then I walk them again after work, and again in the evening before I go to bed. My custom is walk the dogs south in front of the Rust-Not building to an open field where I take them off leash and let them run free.

I was returning from such a walk on the morning that Sandy Springs falsely claims that my dogs attacked him. I had never seen Mr. Springs before this date. I have not had any conversations with him since. I do not understand why he accuses my dogs of attacking him because I saw the entire episode and they did not charge him. They did not bite him. I watched the entire incident, and I am telling the truth.

The dogs were with me on the driveway in front of the Rust-Not building when I first noticed Mr. Springs riding his bicycle. He was riding it on the left or wrong side of the road. He was singing loudly as he approached my dogs. When he saw my dogs, he seemed very frightened. He shouted "damn," real loud, and then began behaving in a very fearful manner. My dogs were attracted first to his loud singing, and then to his shout, so they started to walk slowly toward him.

Then the young man stopped his bicycle, got off it, and began swinging it wildly in the direction of my dogs. He started doing this well before my dogs got close to him. If he was injured, and I seriously doubt that he was, it must have been when he got off his bicycle. He did not do this gracefully. He sort of slammed it to a stop, and then fell forward onto and then off his bike. I noted that his bike did not have a chain guard. If he got cut, he probably cut his leg on one of the chain spokes, or on one of the pedals.

My dogs began circling this guy as he was swinging his bicycle provocatively toward them. My dogs are not accustomed to being threatened, and they were starting to get a bit edgy. They were barking. Dogs bark when they are aroused. They were not baring their teeth. I began to walk rapidly toward the situation because I was afraid this guy might hurt one of my dogs with his bike. I was also a little concerned they might hurt him if he continued provoking them.

I asked him nicely to put his bike down and stop swinging it at my dogs, but he refused. As I got closer, I asked him again. He refused again. I stood there for a few seconds, watching and trying to figure out what to do next. By this time I was so close that I was afraid to reach down and grab my dogs' collars because I was afraid I would get hit by the swinging bike. Finally, the man put down his bike, and I reached out, grabbed my dogs by their collars, and pulled them back toward the driveway.

I saw the entire incident. I was approximately 45 feet away from the man when he got off his bike and my dogs started walking toward him. There was nothing obstructing my view. My dogs never bit him. They never chased him. They never forced him off his bike. This guy's statements to the contrary are lies. I never saw any blood. If my dogs had gone after him like he claims they did, there would have been blood.

After I pulled my dogs away, this guy got on his bike and rode away in a hurry. I watched him ride for awhile. He did not seem to be having any trouble riding his bike. I didn't see any blood dripping from his legs. I don't believe this guy suffered the injuries he claims. If he had, he would not have been able to ride his bike so well. He did stop singing. I was glad about that because he had a lousy voice.

As I turned the corner with my dogs to take them back to my trailer, they briefly took off in the direction this guy had ridden. They did not come within 20 feet of him then, and they stayed on the grass. They never went on the road. As soon as I noticed what had happened, which was in a matter of seconds, I called for them to come. They stopped and trotted back to me. I put them in my trailer and went back to open up Rust-Not because that was my first work responsibility for that day.

I did not hear anything more about this incident until later that afternoon when someone from the Columbia City Health Department came out and asked me some questions about my dogs. I answered them truthfully. Then I received a notice the next day that my dogs were quarantined for a week. I followed all of the instructions I got regarding this quarantine. My dogs did not develop any symptoms of rabies. I keep them on a regular shot program designed to prevent rabies so I was not surprised when there was no problem.

I heard nothing further about this situation until my boss told me he had been sued.

Narrative Summary of Buck Braggart's Deposition

My name is Buck Braggart. I am the manager of the Rust-Not Aluminum Company located at 3426 N.E. 19th Street in Columbia City. This is a branch office of the Rust-Not Aluminum Corporation. The corporation is incorporated in Delaware. Its principal place of business is in Atlanta, Georgia. The corporation has 37 branch stores in Georgia, and it recently has spread to Florida, Tennessee, and Columbia.

Mr. Ted Timid is my personal friend, and also an employee of Rust-Not Aluminum. Mr. Timid's position is that of a clerk-receptionist and general jack of all trades. He works the regular company hours from 8 a.m. to 6 p.m. He is responsible for opening the business in the morning because he lives next door. Two years ago when Ted suffered a series of unexpected financial reversals, I allowed him to move his mobile home onto a vacant lot owned by the company just north of the company's building. Mr. Timid lives there alone.

Mr. Timid is not employed to provide security in any capacity for our business. He completes his working day at 6 p.m. and what he does from then on is his own business. He is not a night watchman. He has no responsibility to check on the building or its premises in evening and early morning hours. His common sense, however, would require him to report anything suspicious that he notices because of his proximity to the building. He is free to come and go when he chooses in the evening, and he has no security assignments.

We do not have a personnel-staffed security system at Rust-Not. Our lot is not fenced. We have a burglar alarm which is connected to a central alarm system monitored by a security office in another location. That person is responsible for notifying the police and me if the alarm sounds in the middle of the evening. Ted is not on the call list. We have had no break-ins or vandalism at the site since we opened. Our stock largely consists of big sheets of aluminum which are not easy to steal or move. This diminishes our need for personnel-based security. We keep no cash on the premises overnight.

I am aware that Ted owns two adult Doberman pincher dogs, and that they live with him as pets. These dogs do not perform any security service for Rust-Not. The Company does not contribute to their care and maintenance. I regard these dogs as Mr. Timid's personal pets. These dogs usually remain in Ted's trailer unless he is walking them. I have seen them walking around the business premises occasionally, and I have never observed them bothering or hassling anyone. My impression of these dogs is that they are very gentle, and that an unprovoked attack by them is extremely unlikely.

Neither me nor Rust-Not has any interest in these dogs. They are not employed by me or by my company, and no aspect of Timid's employment involves these dogs.

IN THE EIGHTH JUDICIAL CIRCUIT COURT OF COLUMBIA IN AND FOR
ALACHUA COUNTY

SANDY SPRINGS

Plaintiff

vs.   Case No.: 12345-CA

RUST NOT ALUMINUM   Division: U
COMPANY
A corporation,
Defendant.

ORDER SETTING PRE TRIAL CONFERENCE

THIS CAUSE coming on this date upon the Court's own motion; and it appearing that said cause is at issue and ready for trial, it is

ADJUDGED that the above styled cause be placed on the calendar for pre-trial conference pursuant to Rule 1.200 of the Columbia Rules of Civil Procedure to consider all matters suggested in said Rule 1.200 to simplify the issues and expedite the trial or other disposition of the case.

It is FURTHER ORDERED as follows:

1. This cause is now set for Jury Trial at the Alachua County Judicial Center, Court Room 2-C, Columbia City, Columbia, in two months.

2. A pre-trial conference in this cause shall be held in two weeks in my chambers, at the Alachua County Judicial Center, Room 201, from 3:00 to 4:30 pm., and that each party shall be represented in said conference by an attorney who expects to conduct the actual trial of the cause.

3. Plaintiff no later than five working days before this pre-trial conference shall file with the Clerk of the Circuit Court and serve a copy on opposing counsel:

   (A) A short statement of the facts on which Plaintiff bases his cause of action.

   (B) An itemized statement of the special damages that Plaintiff expects to prove.

   (C) A schedule of all exhibits and documentary evidence that Plaintiff will offer during trial. (Actual exhibits and documentary evidence must be brought to said conference to facilitate stipulation with respect to authenticity and admissibility.)

   (D) A complete list of witnesses to be used in trial which may not be reopened.

4. Defendant no later than five working days before this pre-trial conference shall file with the Clerk of the Circuit Court and serve a copy on opposing counsel:

(A) The facts constituting the Plaintiffs cause of action which Defendant will admit

(B) If Defendant has filed affirmative defenses or counterclaims, a statement of the facts on which Defendant bases such defenses or counterclaims.

(C) A schedule of all exhibits and documentary evidence that Defendant will offer during trial. Actual exhibits and evidence that Defendant will offer during trial. Actual exhibits and documentary evidence must be brought to said conference to facilitate stipulations regarding authenticity and admissibility.

(D) A complete list of witnesses to be used in trial which may not be reopened.

5. At least one (1) day prior to said conference, trial counsel shall meet or communicate via telephone to discuss settlement in those cases where there has been no negotiation. In those cases in which settlement negotiations have not be instituted, counsel will be prepared to discuss settlement in pre-trial conference and have authority to settle the case or bring to said conference the party or representative who does have authority to act.

6. All proposed jury instructions must be prepared in writing, accompanied by citations of authority, and submitted at this pre-trial conference. There is no need to submit standard jury instructions. No proposed jury instructions will be accepted after this pre-trial conference and the Court will advise counsel shortly before trial begins of its ruling on all proposed jury instructions submitted.

7. All motions in limine must be in writing although they do not need to be briefed. The Court will entertain all written motions in limine at this pre-trial conference filed by 12 noon on the day before this conference.

8. Failure of counsel to comply with the foregoing Court's Order will subject counsel to such penalty as the Court shall determine proper under the circumstances.

DONE AND ORDERED in Chambers at Columbia City, Alachua County, Columbia, this (assume appropriate date).

I.M. *Unfriendly*

Circuit Judge

Copies furnished to:

Counsel for Plaintiff, Abe Aberrant

Counsel for Defendant, Rust-Not Aluminum Co.

EXERCISE 4: JOHN WEBALE v. UNIVERSITY OF WEST DAKOTA [ELECTRONIC DISCOVERY]

FOCUS OF THIS EXERCISE: As associate for outside defense counsel, interview the person who supervised the University's electronic discovery response.

SKILLS INVOLVED: Statutory interpretation, understanding of fundamental electronic discovery concepts and how to apply them to factual situations.

ESTIMATED TIME FOR COMPLETING THIS EXERCISE:

90 minutes

ESTIMATED LEVEL OF DIFFICULTY: Difficult

YOUR ROLE IN THIS EXERCISE: You will play the role either of outside counsel investigating potential issues that have arisen regarding earlier electronic discovery compliance, or the in-house University lawyer who supervised this compliance, at a short conference.

WEBCOURSE FOR EXERCISE 4: Please check the **LexisNexis Webcourse** for additional material that may be posted for this exercise.

EXERCISE 4: JOHN WEBALE v. UNIVERSITY OF WEST DAKOTA

Electronic Discovery Assignment

Assume that you are now a new associate at one of University City's best defense firms, and the only one who can claim expertise dealing with the complications involved in electronic discovery. Your firm has recently been retained by the UWD Attorney to assist in defending John Webale's suit alleging racial discrimination in promotion. Fourteen months have elapsed since Webale filed his complaint, and the deadline for finalizing discovery set in the discovery schedule expires in two months. Your supervising attorney is heading up your firm's participation and has asked you to investigate some apparent problems that have arisen concerning UWD's response to electronic discovery initiated by plaintiff's counsel. She sent you the following email:

Yesterday, as we were preparing for the pre-trial conference, the University Attorney who is assigned to this case said something very disturbing. This alarming remark was that apparently new information has surfaced regarding UWD's earlier responses to focused electronic discovery sought by Webale. Although this lawyer had not reviewed this information, she indicated that it was not helpful to our position. She also said that the new lawyer assigned to supervise this task recently shared this, and that I should get the specifics from that lawyer. By this message I am delegating that task to you, and I think an in person conversation makes the most sense because tact and follow-up may be needed.

I reviewed Webale's production request for electronic information and it looks sound. It seems sufficiently specific in terms of focus and time, i.e. "all documents and other electronic information relating to John Webale's employment at UWD's Fifth Street Parking Ramp, his two promotion efforts in the past two years, and assessments of his candidacy and other candidates for each of these positions." The request to produce defined electronic information to include "email, word processing documents, spreadsheets, presentation documents, graphics, animations, images, audio, video and audiovisual recordings, and voice mail." It included the following platforms in the possession of UWD or third persons under control of UWD such as employees or outside vendors under contract: "databases, networks, computer systems, including legacy systems (hardware and software), servers, archives, back up or disaster recovery systems, tapes, discs, drives, cartridges, and other storage media, laptops, personal computers, internet data, personal digital assistants, hand-held wireless devices, mobile telephones, paging devices, and audio systems including email."

No aspect of this request was objected to or subjected to any review by the presiding Magistrate Judge at the two discovery conferences previously held. UWD filed a response indicating that it had located 27 emails in its systems that fit the request's criteria and would send electronic copies in their native format [with metadata intact] on an agreed upon date. Nothing was deleted or redacted from the electronic copies provided for reasons of privilege or work product. This information was described as descriptive, not analytical, and generally supported the reasons UWD has been maintaining for its promotion decisions.

As far I could glean, no concerns exist about this production, and the issues surround some allegedly "newly discovered" stuff. Your assignment is to learn what this stuff is and make recommendations what we should do next. Given the time limitations facing us, limit your analysis to Rules 26 and 37. Do not do any case-based research at this point.

I am concerned about two possibilities that I want you to investigate fully, and this is where the need for tact enters. The first concerns the effectiveness of UWD's attorney in gathering and preserving electronic evidence in this situation, and the second is spoliation that may have occurred as a result of careless or negligent legal work.

Parties have an obligation to preserve evidence when gaining actual or circumstantial notice that reasonably suggests that this evidence is relevant. The old rules regarding documents and things now govern our digital world where electronically generated and stored information has expanded exponentially, degrades far faster than paper, and is handled by far more persons in entities than used to be the case. Numerous recent opinions hold that litigators cannot rely on the assurances of senior management and in-house counsel concerning e-discovery compliance. District judges and magistrates demand that attorneys who appear before them have enough technical competence through someone on their litigation team to know where the electronic evidence is located and how to preserve, collect, and exchange it in a professionally sound manner. Attorneys, and especially outside counsel like us, are required to understand their client's computer architecture, policies, and actual practices on both a company-wide and user-by-user level. Many, if not most, lawyers today lack the necessary knowledge and skills to fulfill this duty, and have no clue what data retention architecture means, much less how to speak the "geekese" required to talk to IT people who work for their client. Numerous opinions establish that both litigants and their attorneys can be sanctioned for failure to supervise discovery because of the practical reality that discovery is largely run by lawyers and courts and judicial process depend on honesty and fair dealing among attorneys.

Spoliation is the destruction, significant alteration, or failure to preserve evidence for another's use in pending or reasonably foreseeable litigation. As you might expect, this can often happen inadvertently or negligently if electronic discovery is not managed and supervised carefully right from the beginning of, or even before, litigation. Indications that new stuff has been found certainly raises risks that spoliation issues also may be present. Contending with spoliation claims substantially complicates litigation and the harsh sanctions that often result, in addition to their adverse economic effects, are often outcome determinative.

Your assignment is to briefly interview the UWD attorney responsible for managing and supervising the earlier e-discovery response effort.

EXERCISE 5: AMAZING ANALOG v. BELLAGIO INTEGRATED PRODUCTS [DISCOVERY PLANNING NEGOTIATION]

FOCUS OF THIS EXERCISE: As lawyer for either plaintiff or defendant in a trade secrets-breach of contract lawsuit, negotiate before a discovery conference seeking to resolve projected cost and other issues concerning electronically stored information.

SKILLS INVOLVED: Practice rule interpretation, and demonstrate understanding of fundamental discovery planning and cost-shifting provisions in the context of electronically stored information, and how to apply them in developing a stipulated discovery plan.

ESTIMATED TIME FOR COMPLETING THIS EXERCISE:

90 minutes

ESTIMATED LEVEL OF DIFFICULTY: Difficult

YOUR ROLE IN THIS EXERCISE: You will play the role of a lawyer representing either the plaintiff or defendant in a trade-secrets breach of contract law suit, and use confidential information to negotiate a resolution of projected costs and other issues concerning electronically stored information.

WEBCOURSE FOR EXERCISE 5: Please check the **LexisNexis Webcourse** for additional material that may be posted for this exercise.

EXERCISE 5: AMAZING ANALOG, LTD. V. BELLAGIO INTEGRATED PRODUCTS, INC.

Pre-Discovery Conference Planning Negotiation

Plaintiff, Amazing Analog, Ltd. [hereafter AA] is a Columbia corporation which maintains its principal place of business in Greenwich, Columbia. AA designs, manufactures, and markets high-performance analog, mixed signal, and digital signal procession integrated circuits used in signal processing applications. Bellagio Integrated Products, Inc. [BIP] is a West Dakota corporation with its principal place of business in University City, West Dakota. BIP is a competitor of AA, and it is where Chris Michaels, a former employee of AA, is employed. This case was filed in the United States District Court for the Middle District of West Dakota, and involves claims of misappropriation of trade secrets by BIP and Michaels.

AA's complaint alleges that Michaels worked at AA as a design engineer, and signed an agreement when hired that articulated that he would have access to valuable confidential or secret technical and nontechnical information that was vital to AA's success. This agreement also bound Michaels to not disclose to any third party, during the course or after his employment, any proprietary AA data or information, or to use that data or information outside the performance of his job duties. Michaels worked for AA for four years and the complaint alleges that during this time he had access to trade secrets and other confidential information relating to the design, development, implementation, analysis, and fabrication of high speed analog-to-digital converters. Michaels left AA on a Friday six months ago and started working for BIP on the following Monday.

The complaint then alleges that on the night before Michaels resigned from and left AA, he copied a number of schematic drawings that contained trade secrets and related to the design of high speed analog-to-digital converters, and then lied about this copying in his exit interview. The complaint further alleges that Michaels has worked on projects similar to those he participated on at AA, and that he has disclosed and shared AA's trade secret and other confidential information to BIP. The complaint states claims for misappropriation of trade secrets, breach of contract, tort-conversion, unfair competition, and tortuous interference with contract.

BIP answered the complaint by basically admitting Michaels' employment history and denying all allegations of access to and copying and sharing of AA trade secrets and confidential information. The case has been assigned to Magistrate Jon Fitch, a bright man in his early forties who knows more about technology issues than other judges and magistrates in this federal district. Magistrate Fitch has been a very visible and highly vocal advocate of changing the adversarial culture regarding discovery to a more cooperative stance which he claims is particularly needed for electronically stored information [ESI]. In fact, Fitch has been currently lobbying the Middle District of West Dakota to adopt as a local rule the principals of The Sedona Conference Coope ration Proclamation. Key language in this Proclamation states:

> "Lawyers preparing cases for trial need to focus on the full cost of their efforts
> — temporal, monetary, and human. Indeed, all stakeholders in the system —

judges, lawyers, clients, and the general public — have an interest in establishing a culture of cooperation in the discovery process. Over-contentious discovery is a cost that has outstripped any advantage in the face of ESI and the data deluge. It is not in anyone's interest to waste resources on unnecessary disputes, and the legal system is strained by "gamesmanship" or "hiding the ball," to no practical effect. The effort to change the culture of discovery from adversarial conduct to cooperation is . . . an exercise in economy and logic. Establishing a culture of cooperation will channel valuable advocacy skills toward interpreting facts and arguing the appropriate application of law.

Magistrate Fitch has just sent an order scheduling a conference pursuant to Rule 26(f). This exercise assigns you to represent either AA or BIP and then meet and confer to discharge the responsibilities outlined in Rule 26(f)(2) and (3). Your objective is to secure either a stipulation of agreement or a clear statement of opposing views regarding all issues outlined in Rule 26(f)(3). Do not discuss search terms even though this would ordinarily be included in such a conversation. To constrain the scope of this exercise, please limit your conference to the following three discovery issues involving electronically stored information relating to 3 AA high speed analog to digital converter products, called here products 1, 2, and 3, and three allegedly very similar BIP high speed analog to digital converter products, denominated here as 11, 22, and 33. All of these products were placed on the market in the last month:

(1) emails and other ESI in AA's possession that relate to the origination and development of the alleged trade secrets and other confidential information that BIP allegedly misappropriated;

(2) emails and other ESI, in native format relating to the development, design, fabrication, and implementation of 3 BIP high speed analog to digital converter products, labeled here products 11, 22, and 33, which are alleged to be very similar to AA's products 1, 2, and 3; and

(3) All of Michaels' thumb drives and the hard drives of all laptops Michaels owns or possesses, as well as the hard drive of his mother's laptop.

Chapter 9

ADJUDICATION WITHOUT TRIAL

INTRODUCTION

The majority of civil cases in the federal court system do not go to trial. Many of the cases are settled between the parties and many are disposed of through motions which challenge the underlying factual and legal arguments presented. Some early dispositive motions are filed under Rule 12 and attack the validity of specific concepts, such as personal jurisdiction, service of process, and venue. In addition, Rule 12(b)(6) is a device to seek early dismissal of a case when the pleadings themselves do not indicate the plaintiff has stated a claim for relief that is grounded in the law and supported by the facts stated in the complaint. Although cases are dismissed under Rule 12(b)(6), more dispositive motions can be filed later in the case. In this chapter, you will work through exercises on two of those later dispositive motions; the summary judgment motion under Rule 56 and the motion for judgment as a matter of law under Rule 50.

A. Summary Judgment Motions

The motion for summary judgment under Rule 56 is a dispositive motion that can be raised before, during or after discovery. The motion argues that the case should be dismissed because there is "no genuine issue of material fact" and the movant is entitled to judgment as a matter of law. The standard under Rule 56 is not difficult to state but it is difficult to apply and understand. In your Civil Procedure class you may be wondering what the phrase "no genuine issue of material fact" actually means. This phrase is the heart of the summary judgment standard because it highlights what is lacking in the case that makes it appropriate for dismissal — a question of fact in dispute between the parties.

A lawsuit requires two key components; a claim based on valid law and the facts which support the elements of the legal claim. If the case lacks a valid legal basis, the case can be dismissed under Rule 12(b)(6), because that motion disposes of a case when there is no legal claim, regardless of the facts. If the case has a valid legal claim, then the issue turns to whether the facts support the claim. If the facts of the case are not in controversy, there is no question of fact for the fact-finder (the judge in a bench trial or jury in a jury trial). The fact-finder does not need to hear testimony or view exhibits to determine what happened because both parties present the same evidence on the facts. If those agreed upon facts support or do not support the legal claim, the case can be resolved without any work by the fact-finder. A case which can be determined by applying the agreed upon facts to the valid law does not need to go before the fact-finder, thus it can be dismissed through a Rule 56 motion for summary judgment.

Consider this example involving the statute of limitations. Assume plaintiff is filing a lawsuit in a state which observes a two-year statute of limitations in negligence actions. Plaintiff's case seeks damages for personal injury related to an accident which occurred over two years before the filing of your complaint. The date of the accident is noted in the complaint, as is the lawsuit's filing date. Thus, the complaint itself provides facts which show the complaint is filed after the statute of limitations has expired. Assume the defendant asserts the affirmative defense of the statute of limitations. In this case, there is no work for the fact-finder. The facts relevant to the statute of limitations are not in dispute since the plaintiff drafted them into his complaint. The law is not in dispute; therefore there is no genuine issue for a judge or jury. If there is no genuine issue of fact, then the case can be dismissed on summary judgment. The effect of this dismissal is to provide judgment to the defendant as a matter of law.

In working through a problem on summary judgment, you must identify the legal claim at issue and the facts needed to support the claim. Then, you have to analyze which facts are necessary to support your claim and evaluate whether these facts are in dispute. Generally speaking, if the resolution of a fact question relies on calling witnesses to offer testimony and evaluating the credibility of those witnesses, there will be a genuine issue of fact for the fact-finder.

B. Motion for Judgment as a Matter of Law

Motions for Judgment as a Matter of Law (JMOL) under Rule 50 can be used to dispose of a case on similar grounds to the motion for summary judgment. The main difference between a summary judgment motion and the JMOL is timing. A JMOL is appropriate after the trial has begun and can be renewed throughout the trial. The JMOL argues that, based on the evidence presented thus far, no reasonable juror can find in favor of the non-movant and the case should be dismissed. Again, as in summary judgment, the basis of the motion rests on the work required of the fact-finder. When seeking a JMOL, the movant is arguing that based on the evidence presented to the fact-finder, the case should not go forward to verdict.

A JMOL can be made at several points during a trial. The first appropriate opportunity for the motion is typically after the close of the plaintiff's evidence. At this point, the movant argues the jury has now heard all of the plaintiff's evidence and that evidence alone does not support the legal claim, thus the case should not go forward. If the JMOL is denied, the motion can be renewed after the close of the defendant's case. Now the movant is arguing that no reasonable juror can find in favor of the plaintiff based on the plaintiff's evidence and the defendant's evidence. If the judge denies the JMOL at this juncture, the motion can again be renewed after the plaintiff's rebuttal case, if any, or after the case has gone to the jury for verdict. If the motion is made after the jury reaches a verdict, it is sometimes referred to as a Motion for Judgment Notwithstanding the Verdict (JNOV).

The movant on a Motion for Judgment Notwithstanding the Verdict argues that the jury's verdict was not based on the facts and the jury did not deliver a reasoned verdict. If the court grants the JNOV, the case is dismissed despite the jury verdict.

The standard applied in granting the motion is the same standard applied when the motion is made as a JMOL motion earlier in the case. You should note that the parties can only seek a JNOV as a renewal of an earlier JMOL motion. If the party did not make a JMOL motion at trial, he cannot make a JNOV motion after the verdict.

EXERCISE 1: EEC v. TIRES, INC.

FOCUS OF THIS EXERCISE: Dispositive Motions Under Rule 56 (Summary Judgment) and Rule 50 (Motion for Judgment as a Matter of Law).

SKILLS INVOLVED: Reading and understanding the standards applied under Rules 50 and 56; evaluating the facts and evidence available in the case; applying the facts to necessary legal elements of the claim to determine whether the case should be dismissed.

ESTIMATED TIME FOR COMPLETING THE EXERCISE: One to two hours

ESTIMATED LEVEL OF DIFFICULTY: Moderate to difficult.

YOUR ROLE IN THIS EXERCISE: You are playing the role of plaintiff's and defendant's counsel in this exercise.

In Part I of this exercise, the plaintiff has moved the court for summary judgment under Rule 56, arguing that there is no genuine issue of material fact that the defendant failed to exercise safety precautions. You should put yourself in the role of plaintiff's counsel and prepare the argument for summary judgment. In completing Part I of the exercise, please consider the effect of the court granting the plaintiff's motion for summary judgment.

In Part II of this exercise, the defendant has moved the court to dismiss the case at the close of the plaintiff's evidence pursuant to Rule 50. You should put yourself in the role of defendant's counsel and prepare the argument for judgment as a matter of law (JMOL). You should focus on how to structure your argument for judgment as a matter of law based on the facts introduced during the plaintiff's case-in-chief.

EEC Factual Scenario

On February 11, yr-2,[1] a fire started in an industrial park located northwest of Winston-Salem, North Carolina. The fire raged for three full days and ultimately destroyed the facilities and materials belonging to two businesses in the park: EEC (Environmental Ecology Company), a company that filters waste water for reuse in other applications, and Tires, Inc., a company that recycles scrap tires into other products, such as rubber material for the surfaces of athletic fields and play areas. Property loss from the fire is estimated to be in excess of $3,000,000.

It is undisputed that the fire started on the loading dock area of Building G, where both EEC and Tires, Inc. occupied leased space. First attempts to extinguish the fire were made by Tires, Inc. employees. Two employees were operating a forklift and using a pitchfork to move packed tire scraps from a 60x40 foot trailer parked adjacent to the loading dock onto the loading dock. When the employees noticed smoldering and smoke coming from a scrap pile, they began to use a pitchfork to spread the pile of scraps out. According to the fire department investigation report, the smoke ignited into flames when the employees spread the materials out. The ignited fire began to spread, and within 20 minutes, materials on the dock were in flames. An EEC employee noticed the flames through an upstairs window of the EEC plant and called the fire department and police; both arrived within minutes of the call.

The loading dock area was used by both EEC and Tires, Inc. for material and equipment storage. Tires, Inc. stored used tires awaiting recycling and tire scrap on the dock. At the time of the fire, tires and tire scraps covered most of the dock, with used tires piled to heights of 8 feet in certain sections. At the time of the fire, EEC was using a small, rear portion of the dock to store filtration equipment. The loading dock is connected to Building G, which houses Tires, Inc.'s manufacturing facility and EEC's filtration plant and offices. The entire Building G was destroyed in the fire and both companies suffered losses of all their equipment and materials. In addition, both businesses were unable to operate after the fire. Tires, Inc. resumed operations at another facility on August 15, yr-2. EEC is still struggling to reacquire equipment and resume operations. In the months since the fire, many of EEC's clients have taken their business elsewhere and EEC is unsure whether it will be able to rebuild its company and client base. Fortunately, no individuals were harmed in the fire.

EEC has filed suit against Tires, Inc. in the Federal District court for the Middle District of North Carolina for losses sustained in the fire. EEC was insured but the coverage limits on the policy do not cover all of EEC's losses. In its complaint, EEC alleges negligence, stating that the fire resulted from negligent actions related to Tires, Inc.'s recycling processes. According to the complaint, Tires uses a heat based process to remove the steel belts from the rubber tires and that this process generates a large amount of heat. The heat from the process can be held in the scrap rubber for long periods of time if the hot scraps are packed tightly and sealed. EEC alleges that the fire erupted when the stored hot rubber scrap materials were unloaded onto the open-air dock. EEC further alleges that Tires was negligent in not having adequate

---

[1] yr-2 indicates that the year dated is two years ago from the current date. For example if you are working on this exercise in 2014, the fire occurred on Feb 11, 2012.

fire prevention and management materials and practices available to employees when Tires knew it was using a heat based recycling process. According to the complaint, Tires had not installed fire extinguishers or any type of communications equipment on the dock, to be accessed in the event of a fire.

In its answer to EEC's complaint, Tires denies any and all negligence related to the February yr-2 fire. Tires also denies that it owes any duty to EEC as an adjacent tenant in Building G. Furthermore, Tires alleges that EEC was not actively operating at the time of the fire thus they suffered no losses from business interruptions following the fire. Tires also alleges that EEC did not have any equipment stored on the dock at the time of the fire and had equipment of little or no value on the premises of Building G at the time of the fire.

Other relevant facts are as follows:

EEC President: Tom Tuttle

EEC Vice President: Scott Paper

EEC Office Manager: Beth Brett

EEC Equipment Foreman and Facilities Supervisor: Pete Preston

Tires President: Quinn Quincy

Tires Vice President: Ralph Ready

Tires Plant Manager: Mark McGhee

W-S Fire Dept. Chief: Denis Leary

EXERCISE 1: EEC v. TIRES, INC.

Part I: Summary Judgment

Plaintiffs assume the following re status of the case:

The parties are nearing the end of the discovery period and will soon schedule the pre-trial conference. All of the relevant witnesses have been deposed and each side has information gained through Interrogatories and Requests for Production of Documents. The Tires, Inc. employees have testified in deposition that there have been other fires at Tires, Inc. caused by hot rubber scrap, and the Fire Department records show three 911 calls for small fires in the 2 years prior to the fire that harmed EEC. On the prior fire reports and on two prior fire inspections, the absence of fire equipment was noted by the Fire Department. There is no evidence of any fire prevention equipment on the loading dock in the three years prior to the fire or at the time of the fire.

Assume North Carolina substantive law requires a commercial tenant to ensure the safety of the leased premises by installing fire prevention equipment, in the absence of a contract placing that responsibility on the landlord. EEC acquired copies of the Tires, Inc. lease in discovery, and the lease did not require the landlord to install fire prevention equipment in Building G or the adjacent loading dock. Also, local ordinances require fire extinguishers in any area where combustible materials are stored.

Based on the uncontroverted evidence that Tires, Inc. did not have any fire prevention equipment on the dock, EEC now wants to move the Court for partial summary judgment on the claim that Tires, Inc. is liable for failure to have fire equipment on the dock. EEC's theory is that the availability of fire prevention or safety equipment would have, at a minimum, prevented the fire from consuming the loading dock and Building G areas which housed EEC property and operations. If the motion is granted, the only liability issue at trial will be negligence in the storage and handling of the combustible materials.

Prepare to argue the Motion for Partial Summary Judgment representing EEC, the movant.

Webcourse for Exercise 1, Part 1:

In preparing your motion, refer to Rule 56 of the Federal Rules of Civil Procedure. You may also want to access the Review Podcast on Summary Judgment which is available on the **LexisNexis Webcourse** that was created for this book.

EXERCISE 1: EEC v. TIRES, INC.

Part 2: Summary Judgment

Defendants assume the following re status of the case:

The parties are nearing the end of the discovery period and will soon schedule the pre-trial conference. All of the relevant witnesses have been deposed and each side has information gained through Interrogatories and Requests for Production of Documents. Despite discovery requests, EEC has failed to produce any invoices or receipts verifying the existence of the property allegedly destroyed by the fire. EEC has produced an inventory created by an EEC manager, Pete Preston, after the fire. Preston's inventory is based on his memory of what was on the dock. EEC has also produced pictures of certain pieces of equipment allegedly stored on the dock, but there is no way to verify the pictures were taken of EEC equipment or that it was in the location of the fire. Also, due to the nature of the fire, there is no evidence at the site of what exactly was stored on the EEC portion of the dock.

The North Carolina substantive law of damages requires the plaintiff to provide documentary evidence of lost property in an action claiming damages for lost property. It is not enough for a witness to testify as to what property was lost in a fire. The plaintiff must be able to document the loss by some other means in order to recover the replacement value of the property.

Tires, Inc. now wants to file a Motion for Summary Judgment arguing there is no genuine issue of material fact that Plaintiff EEC cannot recover lost property damages when they have failed to produce the necessary documentary evidence in discovery. It is Tires, Inc.'s theory that EEC did not have property stored on the loading dock at the time of the fire. Through the summary judgment motion, Tires, Inc. will argue all of EEC's claims related to property stored on the loading dock should be dismissed because EEC cannot prove damages, an essential element of the negligence claims.

Prepare the argument for the Tires, Inc. motion.

Webcourse for Exercise 1, Part 2:

In preparing your motion, refer to Rule 56 of the Federal Rules of Civil Procedure. You may also want to access the Review Podcast on Summary Judgment which is available on the **LexisNexis Webcourse** that was created for this book.

EXERCISE 2: EEC v. TIRES, INC.

PART II: MOTION FOR JUDGMENT AS A MATTER OF LAW

Defendants review Part 2 of the Summary Judgment Exercise and assume the following:

The defendant's motion for summary judgment on the element of damages was denied and the case proceeds to trial. At trial, the plaintiffs have still failed to produce documentary evidence of the property lost in the fire. During the plaintiff's case-in-chief, the plaintiff called the following witnesses to testify to the damages element:

- Tom Tuttle, EEC President and Scott Paper, EEC Vice President both testified to the existence of equipment on the loading dock at the time of the fire but could not specify what equipment was being stored on the dock or anything about the value or condition of that equipment.

- Beth Brett, EEC Office Manager, testified that the office in Building G contained miscellaneous office equipment but nothing of great value. She did not know the location of any inventories, documents, or receipts verifying the existence of the equipment allegedly located on the loading dock. Also, she testified she had no personal knowledge of any equipment stored on the loading dock at the time of the fire.

- Pete Preston, EEC Equipment Foreman and Facilities Supervisor, was the Plaintiff's key witness on damages. Preston produced an inventory of the equipment located on the loading dock at the time of the fire. He testified that the inventory was based on his memory of what was stored on the dock and was created after the fire. Preston's inventory does not include detailed information about the equipment, such as serial numbers, acquisition dates, or depreciation and use information. Also, Preston testified that he had not checked on the loading dock equipment for two weeks or longer before the fire and acknowledged the possibility that the inventory of equipment could have changed in the time between when he last checked the stored equipment and the time of the fire. Preston was also able to produce photos of some of the equipment he remembers was stored on the dock but could not testify to when the photos were taken and whether the equipment allegedly lost in the fire was exactly the same equipment in the photographs.

- Fire Department Investigator Jim Jones testified that the fire was an extremely hot and destructive fire fueled by petroleum-based rubber. He also testified that in his post-fire investigations, he was unable to locate the remains of any specific pieces of property on the loading dock. In Jones's expert opinion, it would be impossible to prove what items were stored on the loading dock through the fire investigation of this type of fire.

- Plaintiff did not offer any evidence regarding the fair market value of the property allegedly lost in the fire.

At the close of plaintiff's evidence, defendant Tires, Inc. moves the court for Judgment as a Matter of Law under Rule 50, arguing that the plaintiff has failed to prove the essential element of damages, thus no reasonable juror could find in plaintiff's favor on the issue of negligence. As counsel for the defendant, prepare an outline of your motion argument.

Webcourse for Exercise 2:

In preparing your motion, refer to Rule 50 of the Federal Rules of Civil Procedure. You may also want to access the Review Podcast on Summary Judgment and Rule 50 Motions which is available on the **LexisNexis Webcourse** that was created for this book.

Chapter 10

THE PRE-TRIAL CONFERENCE REQUIREMENT

INTRODUCTION

Planning skills, encompassing identifying proof needs, probable discovery methods and problems, and strategic thinking regarding how to present preferred positions in negotiations and judicial interactions, are important earlier than they used to be in civil lawsuits. This is because lawyers handling civil claims and defenses increasingly confront required interactions with judges, magistrates, and counterparts early and often. Judicial interventions designed to manage cases are authorized by two Federal Rules, 16 and 26(f). These interactions encompass planning and resolving issues concerning pleadings, discovery, pre-trial dispositive motions, and trial matters. The broad expansion of Rule 16 in 1983 was designed to expand pre-trial conferencing to establish early and continuing judicial management, discourage wasteful pretrial activities, and facilitate settling cases.

The impact of these rules encourages lawyers to think carefully about their cases much earlier in litigation than many did previously. This short timetable encourages lawyers to engage in prompt researching law, canvassing information on hand, identifying discovery needs and probable sources of that information, and considering how best to obtain needed data. Usually before formal discovery begins, lawyers must meet and confer to plan discovery, submit a written report to the judge, and attend a pretrial scheduling conference.

This meet and confer interaction should occur "as soon as practicable" under Rule 26(f)(1), and at least 21 days before a scheduling conference is held or order is due. While lawyers need to know when their judge has or tends to set scheduling conference dates, this usually occurs when all important parties have answered. Local court rules and individual standing orders of Judges must be consulted. Discovery plans should include changes to and timing of initial mandated disclosures; subjects, timing, and order of other anticipated discovery; modifications of discovery limits in the federal and local court rules; and needs for protective orders. Careful planning is particularly important in identifying and suggesting resolutions to potential issues raised by identifying, preserving, searching, and preserving electronically stored information.

Unresolved discovery plan disputes should be noted in the report submitted to the judge before the discovery conference. Adopted discovery plans typically become part of the Judge's scheduling order that control lawsuits. This scheduling order establishes deadlines for filing motions, amending pleadings, and completing discovery. These deadlines can be changed only with good cause. Additional pretrial conferences are often needed to manage expert and electronically stored discovery issues, and to prepare for the unlikely events of actual trials. Rule 16(c) permits additional pretrial case management conferences whenever judges convene them, and lists 16 topics for consideration at these sessions. Decisions that result from these meetings are written into case management orders. Implementing these procedures for informal and formal meetings to discuss needs and concerns benefits from actions that are cooperative and efficient. Choosing to act contentiously and unreasonably often earns judicial ire and sanctions.

Overarching all case management is the direction that judges assist settlement at every junction. Judicial assistance usually encourages judicial encouragement and many worry that the line between encouragement and coercion sometimes blurs. Studies suggest most judges stop short of suggesting a numeric figure as the appropriate settlement point. Other empirical evidence suggests that judges with the highest rates of settlement are those who move cases quickly by setting and enforcing firm deadlines and trial dates. Enforcing discovery deadlines also tends to ensure settlement of cases.

The rules provide nothing to guide judicial discretion whether or not to use any specific case management technique, and appellate courts reverse their decisions only for abusing discretion. Important procedural decisions are made in this context. Anecdotal and experimental data show that different case management choices dramatically affect and alter outcomes. Critics contend that intensive case management requires judges to start making outcome-affecting decisions early based on limited information, and departs from the adversarial ideal of shielding ultimate decision-makers from early exposure to evidence and arguments.

Lawyers use negotiation and persuasion skills to navigate these uncertain, fluid, and highly context-dependent arenas. This requires realizing that adversarial battle attaches to trial while most judges view pre-trial as a problem-solving exercise requiring reasonable give and take. Effective actions usually results from cooperative language, tone, and pace choices; prompt, comprehensive preparation of legitimate pre-trial process needs; and focus on interests underlying legal positions. Effective negotiating and persuading in these contexts also often requires willingness to trade low value concerns in return for concessions that matter more; openness to creative, flexible solutions; and concise presentations of persuasive reasons, based on objective standards to the maximum possible extent, that judges should agree with their views on contested issues.

EXERCISE 1: YOU WANT ME TO DO WHAT?

FOCUS OF THIS EXERCISE: Counseling a client about a settlement offer opposing counsel made at a pre-trial conference and then reiterated in an offer of judgment under a fictitiously amended FRCP Rule 68.

SKILLS INVOLVED: Practicing rule interpretation and client-centered counseling regarding how to respond to a settlement proposal made in a formal offer of judgment in an ethically challenging context.

ESTIMATED TIME FOR COMPLETING THIS EXERCISE:

45 minutes

ESTIMATED LEVEL OF DIFFICULTY: Moderate

YOUR ROLE IN THIS EXERCISE: You will play the role of either the lawyer or client in a short conference to discuss how to respond to a settlement proposal made in a formal offer of judgment suggested by the presiding judge at the pre-trial conference.

WEBCOURSE FOR EXERCISE 1: Please check the **LexisNexis Webcourse** for additional material that may be posted for this exercise.

Chapter 11

JOINDER

PART I:
ADDING PARTIES AND CLAIMS TO THE LAWSUIT

INTRODUCTION

Lawyers representing plaintiffs must apply procedural knowledge and tactical thinking when they assess two important issues when sculpting their lawsuit. This chapter analyzes only these decisions. Our adversarial system affords rights to joined defendants to make claim and party joinder decisions, and the issues these procedural devices generate are covered elsewhere. The plaintiffs' initial issues encompass what claims and parties should, and must, be joined together in this litigation. Making these choices effectively requires integrating substantive and procedural knowledge, careful planning, and effective strategic thinking. They require anticipating pleading battles, discovery issues, summary judgment risks, trial persuasion challenges, and potential post-trial preclusion effects.

Federal rules regulating claims allow joining against opposing parties as many claims as lawyers can find in applicable law applied to clients' facts and objectives. These claims can be either independent or alternative. They certainly should include all claims related to core events and their underlying facts that are needed to protect and advance client interests and objectives, assuming that federal subject matter jurisdictional rules discussed elsewhere are met.

This claim joinder freedom brings risk that doctrines of claim preclusion may bar post-trial efforts to litigate claims that could and should have been brought initially. Contemporary law defines claims broadly to encompass virtually everything that attaches to specific events and the facts embodied in these occurrences. Adding additional, unrelated claims raises less preclusion risks but makes cases more complex, broadens discovery's scope potentially increasing its time and expense, and may require adding additional parties which also expands complexity and cost. Thinking through trial objectives to develop a case theory often helps lawyers make this assessment skillfully. Winning trial stories are typically based on facts, not law; and they are bolstered by organizing credible witnesses and believable evidence to win the war over disputed facts by presenting more persuasive proof than counterparts muster.

Determining who to join as defendants requires equally careful thought. Leaving aside required party joinder, a topic covered elsewhere, federal practice regarding permissive selection of parties is less expansive than claim joinder. It requires a transaction relationship, allowing plaintiffs to join multiple defendants, or to join together, only if claims arise out of the same transaction, occurrence, or series of occurrences, and have at least one common question of law or fact. This narrower scope to join acknowledges the complexity of adding parties which increase cost, time, and risk jury confusion and inaccuracy. Post-trial preclusion impacts party joinder less because of the due process tenet that later litigation cannot generally preclude persons were not involved in the earlier lawsuit [with exceptions for privity and representational statuses]. Judges retain power to divide claims, parties, or both into separately tried cases.

Lawyers determining whether to join parties who could be brought into the lawsuit permissively must skillfully assess a wide range of tactical factors. These include judgment collection implications; expanded discovery opportunities from enlarging the reach of tools that include parties; increased discovery costs, delays, and quarrels; the risks of adding better or more contentious opposing counsel; balancing the risks of acquiring divide and conquer strategies against facing coalition-based defenses; anticipated negotiation and mediation consequences; and potential decision-maker impacts.

EXERCISE 1: MUSICAL CHAIRS

FOCUS OF THIS EXERCISE: Interpret applicable rule provisions and a complex federal statute and interview an expert witness hired by client.

SKILLS INVOLVED: Use rule provisions and statutory guidelines to guide investigation interview.

ESTIMATED TIME FOR COMPLETING THIS EXERCISE:

60 minutes

ESTIMATED LEVEL OF DIFFICULTY: Somewhat difficult

YOUR ROLE IN THIS EXERCISE: You play the role of either a lawyer investigating suing University students for illegal file sharing or an expert witness hired by the client, and do a short interview to assess procedural options.

WEBCOURSE FOR EXERCISE 1: Please check the **LexisNexis Webcourse** for additional material that may be posted for this exercise.

EXERCISE 1:   MUSICAL CHAIRS

Joinder Investigation

You are a brand new associate working in the litigation department of University City's largest law firm. Your supervising senior associate recently sent you the following e-mail. After reading it, your task is to conduct the assigned interview.

To: You

From: Supervising Senior Associate

Subject: Needed investigation, analysis, and recommendations

CONFIDENTIAL: FOR IN-FIRM DISTRIBUTION ONLY

We have been approached by a consortium of sixteen record companies who own or license copyrights issued by the United States government. They wish to sue nineteen students currently enrolled at the University of West Dakota for copyright infringement arising from alleged dissemination of plaintiff's copyrighted sound recordings over the Internet on a peer-to-peer [P2P] filing system. A P2P network is an online media distribution system that allows users to transform their computers into an interactive internet site and disseminate files for other users to copy. The sixteen record companies want to claim that their exclusive rights under the Federal Copyright Act include the exclusive rights to reproduce the copyrighted recordings and to distribute these works to the public. They want statutory damages pursuant to 17 U.S.C. § 504(c) for each infringement by each defendant of each copyrighted recording. They also want us to reimburse as much of our fees as the Court deems reasonable and costs pursuant to 17 U.S.C. § 505.

The true identity of each defendant is not known to the consortium at this time so they seek to join them as Doe defendants. [Assume that Federal practice permits this in appropriate contexts, and this is one] P2P users who disseminate (upload) and who copy (download) copyrighted material violate the Federal copyright laws. *A&M Records, Inc. v. Napster, Inc.*, 239 F.3d 1004, 1013-14 (9th Cir. 2001); *In re Aimster Copyright Litigation*, 334 F.3d 643 (7th Cir. 2003), *cert denied*, 124 S. Ct. 1069 (2004).

The consortium has completed an intensive investigation that proves that each of the 19 identified accounts is an active participant in the Dark Shadow network, the largest current P2P network. Consequently, each account has apparently participated in an online swap meet, offering copyrighted sound recordings for download to other users, and downloading copyrighted sound recordings from other users. This investigation suggests that each account has apparently made available hundreds of thousands of copyrighted sound recordings unlawfully, and in exchange for the chance to copy millions of files illegally copied and disseminated by others.

When using P2P networks, participants typically use user names and not their true names. Our client's investigation can identify the Internet Protocol (IP) address from which each account was unlawfully disseminating copyrighted works, but could not ascertain the actual name, address, or any other contact information for anyone using these accounts. Using these IP addresses, the investigation determined that Open House Networks (OHN), an Internet Service Provider (ISP) who serves the central West Dakota region, serves each implicated IP. OHN provides service by contract to the University of West Dakota (UWD) who then provides IP addresses to its students. A code added to each UWD account holder indicates that all nineteen of these accounts fall within UWD's contract with OHN. Our investigation further revealed that OHN's contract with UWD subjects it to all confidentiality obligations that bind UWD.

The Family Educational Rights and Privacy Act, 20 U.S.C. § 1232g grants privacy rights to students attending educational institutions or agencies that receive federal funds. UWD receives extensive federal funding. Subsection (b)(2)(B) of this Act prohibits receiving federal funds if educational institutions or agencies have a policy or practice of "releasing, or providing access to, any personally identifiable information in education records other than directory information, as is permitted in paragraph (1) of this section, unless:

(A)   there is written consent from the student's parents specifying records to be released, the reasons for such release, and to whom, and with a copy of the records to be released to the student's parents and the student if desired by the parents, or

(B)   except as provided in paragraph (1)(J), such information is furnished in compliance with judicial order, or pursuant to any lawfully issued subpoena, upon condition that parents and the students are notified of all such orders or subpoenas in advance of the compliance therewith by the educational institution or agency.

Paragraph (1) of section (b) of this same Act prohibits federal funding if educational institutions or agencies have "a policy or practice of permitting the release of education records (or personally identifiable information contained therein other than directory information, as defined in paragraph (5) of subsection (a) of this section) of students without the written consent of their parents to any individual, agency, or organization, other than to the following [and then several subsections follow]."

One of these subsections, (1)(J)(ii) authorizing release to "the entity or persons designated in any other subpoena issued for a law enforcement purpose, in which case the court or other issuing agency may order, for good cause shown, the educational agency or institution (and any officer, director, employee, agent, or attorney for such agency or institution) on which the subpoena is served, to not disclose to any person the existence or contents of the subpoena or any information furnished in response to the subpoena." [FYI, (1)(J)(i) deals with Federal grand jury subpoenas and criminal investigations.]

Finally, paragraph (a)(5)(A) of this same Act defines the phrase "directory information relating to a student" to include: "the student's name, address, telephone listing, date and place of birth, major field of study, participation in officially recognized activities and sports, weight and height of members of athletic teams, dates of attendance, degrees and awards received, and the most previous educational agency or institution attended by the student."

I need you to interview the lead investigator for this consortium and determine whether we can join these plaintiffs, these claims, and these account owners as John Doe defendants in a copyright infringement suit filed in the United States District Court for the Central District of West Dakota [where UWD is located]. This investigator is not a lawyer and has not worked on similar matters in the past.

PART II:
JURISDICTIONAL ISSUES CREATED BY JOINDER

Introduction

When adding parties to a lawsuit in federal court through the mechanisms of party joinder, you must also consider the rules of subject matter jurisdiction. If the defendant adds another defendant to the lawsuit through Rule 14 impleader and the added defendant is not diverse from the plaintiff, can this destroy the subject matter jurisdiction of a case properly brought under diversity of citizenship? In your Civil Procedure course, you may have discussed this joinder-related issue under the title supplemental jurisdiction.

Supplemental jurisdiction resides at the intersection between subject matter jurisdiction and joinder. For this reason, your Civil Procedure course may discuss supplemental jurisdiction in either or both parts of the course. Regardless of where the topic fits into your course, the core issue in supplemental jurisdiction is consistent. When analyzing a supplemental jurisdiction question, you are asking whether the court can take subject matter jurisdiction over additional claims and parties added to a lawsuit when the lawsuit, in its form after joinder, does not meet the requirements of subject matter jurisdiction.

To understand supplemental jurisdiction, you should examine it in a factual context. Assume Jay has sued David in federal court in New York under a federal fraud statute. The case is properly in federal court under federal question jurisdiction. Now assume that David adds a counterclaim for defamation, a state law claim, against Jay. If the case is in federal court based only on the federal question, can the federal court maintain subject matter jurisdiction when a state claim is added? The answer to this question evokes all the joy and aggravation of law school: maybe.

The case law story for supplemental jurisdiction starts in 1966 in the case *United Mine Workers v. Gibbs*,[1] when the Supreme Court held that a federal court can take supplemental jurisdiction over a joined claim when both claims "derive from a common nucleus of operative fact." So if Jay's fraud claim and David's defamation claim both arise from "a common nucleus of operative fact," the federal court can take subject matter jurisdiction over the state law claim.

The *Gibbs* test was the standard until twenty-three years later, when the Supreme Court revisited the supplemental jurisdiction test of *Gibbs* in two later cases. In *Finley v. United States*,[2] the plaintiff sued several defendants, including the FAA and the local government, after she lost her husband and children in a plane crash. The plaintiff alleged that the FAA was negligent in not maintaining a safe airport and further alleged that the local government which owned the airport was negligent for allowing utility lines too close to the airport. The claim against the FAA was properly

---

[1] *United Mine Workers of America v. Gibbs*, 388 U.S. 715 (1966).

[2] *Finley v. United States*, 490 U.S. 545 (1989).

in federal court under the Federal Tort Claims Act (FTCA). The claim against the local government and other local defendants was not properly in federal court on either federal question or diversity grounds. Although the claims derived from a "common nucleus of operative fact," the Supreme Court did not allow for supplemental jurisdiction in Ms. Finley's tragic case. The Supreme Court was uncomfortable using the *Gibbs* test when the result was to destroy the cardinal rule of complete diversity.

In *Owen Equipment and Erection Co. v. Kroger,*[3] Mrs. Kroger, domiciled in Iowa, sued the Omaha Public Power District (OPPD) for the wrongful death of her husband. OPPD had its principal place of business in Nebraska, and the case went to federal court on diversity. OPPD then joined another defendant, Owen Equipment and Electric Co.(Owen). OPPD was subsequently removed from the case, leaving only Mrs. Kroger and Owen. Everything would have been fine were it not for the fact that, much to everyone's surprise[4], Owen's principal place of business was in Iowa. The Supreme Court determined that the District Court no longer had the power to hear the case because diversity was destroyed. The Court recognized that there must not only be the constitutional power to hear the case (arising from Article III, Section 2), statutory power must exist as well. According to the Supreme Court, if Congress had intended for Mrs. Kroger's situation to be allowed in federal court, they should have made a rule addressing that situation.

The stories of *Finley* and *Kroger* serve as great examples of how the law can and should evolve. In sum, the Supreme Court told Congress that the issue of altering or preserving the rule of complete diversity was a statutory matter. Congress listened and followed these cases with the creation of 28 U.S.C. § 1367. Section 1367 is now the controlling authority for supplemental jurisdiction questions. Supplemental jurisdiction questions raised by claim or party joinder must be analyzed through 28 U.S.C. § 1367. Therefore, the most important practical aspect of this topic for law students is the ability to analyze a supplemental jurisdiction question under Section 1367.

---

[3] *Owen Equipment and Erection Co. v. Kroger*, 437 U.S. 365 (1978).

[4] The change in principal place of business from Nebraska to Iowa was due to accretion in the Missouri river through the town of Carter Lake, Iowa, which relocated the state line, thus changing Owen's domicile.

EXERCISE 2: UNDERSTANDING THE STATUTORY ANALYSIS

FOCUS OF THIS EXERCISE: The focus of this exercise is for you to understand the process of analyzing a supplemental jurisdiction question under Section 1367.

SKILLS INVOLVED: Legal analysis and statutory construction.

ESTIMATED TIME FOR COMPLETING THE EXERCISE:

30 minutes

ESTIMATED LEVEL OF DIFFICULTY: Moderate

YOUR ROLE IN THIS EXERCISE: In this exercise, you should assume you have been asked by a fellow student to explain the analytical process under Section 1367. Use the flow chart and other materials provided to analyze the factual problem step by step. You can analyze the problem orally, working alone or with another student, or you can attempt to write out an analysis as you would an exam answer.

WEBCOURSE FOR THE EXERCISE:

As you analyze this exercise, you will need to access the Supplemental Jurisdiction Flow Chart included on the **LexisNexis Webcourse** that was created for this book. You may also want to review 28 U.S.C. § 1367, available through LexisNexis.

EXERCISE 2:   UNDERSTANDING THE STATUTORY ANALYSIS

Assume John, a resident of Hawaii, is involved in an auto accident with Kate, a resident of Maine, while Kate is driving a rental van on vacation in Hawaii. John is seriously hurt in the accident and suffers medical damages in excess of $100,000. John sues Kate in federal court in Hawaii claiming negligence. The lawsuit is properly in federal court under diversity jurisdiction.

After John commenced the lawsuit against Kate, he discovered there had been another passenger in Kate's van at the time of the accident. This passenger, Alan, had encouraged Kate's unusually reckless driving and had intentionally distracted Kate while she was driving on the treacherous island roads. Alan resides in Hawaii. Worried that Kate may not be able to pay his expensive medical debt, John wants to add Alan as a defendant but Alan and John are not diverse.

Will the Federal Court be able to take supplemental jurisdiction over John's claim against Alan?